Lancashire

Edited by Steve Twelvetree

Young**Writers**
First published in Great Britain in 2006 by:
Young Writers
Remus House
Coltsfoot Drive
Peterborough
PE2 9JX
Telephone: 01733 890066
Website: www.youngwriters.co.uk

SB ISBN 1 84602 369 6

Foreword

This year, the Young Writers' *POP! - The Power Of Poetry* competition proudly presents a showcase of the best poetic talent selected from thousands of up-and-coming writers nationwide.

Young Writers was established in 1991 to promote the reading and writing of poetry within schools and to the young of today. Our books nurture and inspire confidence in the ability of young writers and provide a snapshot of poems written in schools and at home by budding poets of the future.

The thought, effort, imagination and hard work put into each poem impressed us all and the task of selecting poems was a difficult but nevertheless enjoyable experience.

We hope you are as pleased as we are with the final selection and that you and your family continue to be entertained with *POP! Lancashire* for many years to come.

Contents

Walshaw High School

The Poems

The Power Of Mother Nature

Ocean.
Vast, arms open wide.
Ready to swallow,
Anything that falls in its realms.
Man.
Possesses knowledge.
Knowledge of Mother Nature
And her powers of constructing,
The tallest tree and the prettiest flower,
But not enough knowledge of her power to destroy.
Destruction beyond human control.
Wave.
Advances towards the land.
A wall of water tumbles the land.
A wall of water tumbles and crashes its way,
Onto man's paradise on Earth.
Paradise.
Turns into the complete opposite.
Man.
Knows not what to do.
Immense numbers suffer,
At the hands of Mother Nature
And in the distance
A small boy weeps.
Along with thousands more across the globe,
At the thought of loved ones,
Who will never be seen alive.
Again.

Mrinalini Dey (14)

Miss Nice

Miss Nice is ever so mean,
To give out detentions, she's ever so keen.
With her long nails as sharp as a sword,
They glisten and gleam against the whiteboard.

She stares at you as though you're a snake,
Her lessons are like drowning in a lake.
Her voice echoes through the school,
Even wakes up the basement ghoul.

She can hear the wind trickling from the class tap,
If you aren't careful, you're in for a slap.
Her haunting shadow will frighten you away,
Especially in the daunting month of May.

Her nose is as pointed as a carrot
And when she speaks she sounds just like a parrot.
Her eyes remind me of a two-foot black rat,
Which makes no difference, because she looks like a cat.

You can see the saliva dripping down her mouth
And her gungy bogies head for south.
Her revolting hair is filled with nits,
You can see them crawling as she sits.

Her ears stick out like an elf's
And it looks even bigger when she stands by the shelf.
Her footsteps leave giant prints behind,
She won't dare to think of anyone kind.

You can hear her croaking voice from miles away,
Her hair looks like it's made from hay.
Everyone fears to say a word to Miss Nice,
They all make sure they act like mice.

She carries a wrinkled stick wherever she goes
And holds it so it's just below her nose.
Overall, Miss Nice is a teacher you should dread,
This is what all the students have said.

Hadeal Jaidy (13)
Ashton Community Science College

Hallowe'en

Dressing up and eating things sweet,
Meeting vampires down the street.
Candy apples as red as blood,
Hallowe'en is never a dud.

The Dracula Mansion is the scariest thing,
I hear clanging and things cackling.
The windows are as black as the night,
But on All Hallows Eve they're filled with fright.

A family of ghosts live just next door,
They're almost as scary or even more.
Birds go *squawk* and dogs go *bark,*
As kids run screaming in the dark.

The lonely scarecrow that longs for a friend,
Goes slowly walking on times depend.
Wading and squelching through the mud,
For just as long as he should.

The scary-looking pumpkins are all alight,
Keeping all things filled with fright.
For in the morning when kids wake up,
It won't happen again till a year is up.

Karis Jade Treuberg (13)
Ashton Community Science College

All Hallows Eve

Hallowe'en is near,
Time for trick or treat,
Seeing friends down the road,
You don't know who you'll meet.

Hallowe'en is near,
Pumpkins glowing in the night,
A bunch of them in the street,
You're sure to have a fright.

Hallowe'en is near,
Full of scary costumes,
Looking up in the sky,
You can smell witches' perfumes.

Hallowe'en is near,
Flying ever so high,
Witches with broomsticks,
High in the sky.

Hallowe'en is near,
Lots of ghostly fun,
Watch behind you,
Quick, quick, run!

Hallowe'en is near,
We love it so much,
When ghostly fingers,
Reach out to touch.

Lucy Earl (12)
Ashton Community Science College

It Will Never Be The Same Again

The sky darkened like the switch of a light,
A blanket covered with all its might.
The World Trade Center was no more,
As the invasion of evil opened its door.

People were running, broken and bare,
Whoever did this, did not care.
I looked on the floor and couldn't believe,
What my eyes saw, I wanted to leave.

Joy and laughter, I could not hear,
Replaced by the sound of sadness and fear.
The stench of broken bodies filled the air,
To turn back and look, I did not dare.

We've got to be brave now in the dark days ahead,
To love one another as the Bible said.
It's going to be hard after all the talk,
We'll put our hands together and pray for New York.
Men, women and children hurting inside,
All those innocent people should never have died.
God will be with us, I know that's a fact,
Places of worship, forever will be packed.

Bridie Conboy (16)
Blackpool Sixth Form College

Lover's Confusion

Emotionless emotions
Give me feelings that aren't felt,
As a final, lonely tear,
Dries my empty eyes.
Wordless words
You heard when you were deaf,
Mean meaningless things
Which mean much to me.
Confused in all my certainty;
What was wrong, felt right.
As I stumble in my confidence
And lose, yet win a friend.
Closer, but so far away,
Although you are so near.
Ripping through my heart you go,
A soft and tender spear.

Aimée Spinks (16)
Blackpool Sixth Form College

Vampire Hotel

Vampires strike at night,
In the deadly, darkened sky,
They are as quick as light,
They don't show themselves much,
At vampire hotel.

They have teeth as sharp as knives,
They screech like bats in the darkened sky,
They creep through the rooms of a silent house,
At vampire hotel.

The flickering of flames of the hotel fire,
In the deadly silence,
Lays a dog awake waiting for the vampires to strike,
Waiting, waiting,
At vampire hotel.

Kathy Moore (12)
Burscough Priory Science College

The Ride In The Executioner's Wagon

The cart's crooked wheels screeched,
As tree roots reared out of the mud like gnarled hands,
Whilst they drove through the ravine,
The horse's hooves *clip-clopped,*
As thunder growled
And lightning pierced the night sky.

'Igor lives in the castle,'
He replied to Hannah's question,
'In which part?' she asked.
He said, 'It's warmest in the kitchen.'
The horse's hooves *clip-clopped,*
As thunder growled
And lightning pierced the night sky.

Raindrops came straight through her umbrella
And settled like a mist over her.
The horse reared and neighed
And a flash of lightning illuminated the castle.
The horse's hooves *clip-clopped,*
As the thunder growled
As lightning pierced the night sky.

'The werewolf terrified all the village folk,'
Said Igor, with a croak.
'Count Dracula left the castle
And took away a great deal of hassle.'
The horse's hooves didn't *clip-clop,*
Because they had arrived.

Alex Clark (12)
Burscough Priory Science College

Hurricane Katrina

In New Orleans the town's awake,
Because they know it's too late,
To run away,
From their terrible fate.

The wind blows high,
The wind blows low,
The wind blows fast,
The wind blows slow.

The levees were breached,
The water leaked in,
While the people screeched,
The destruction begins.

The storm had lifted,
It had gone away,
But in New Orleans,
They'll remember this day.

Callum Alexander Thow (12)
Burscough Priory Science College

Left Behind

Sydney is the place to be,
With clear blue skies and a deep blue sea,
On board the 'Sea-Esta' for a diving trip,
With a friendly skipper to give us a tip.

Down in the blue with the wonderful fish,
But for this to go right, you would have to wish,
Strong currents came and pulled me away,
When I resurfaced I could not see day.

With barely an hour till night-time fell,
I waved at ships but they could not tell,
Sharks were passing around my feet,
Those creatures I wish I won't have to meet.

Night-time has fallen and all hope is lost,
Until the skipper comes back at no cost,
'You were freakishly lucky,' the skipper said to me,
I don't think I'll ever go back in the sea.

Ella Oakley (12)
Burscough Priory Science College

9/11

There were the two towers standing bright,
The big symbol of the New York skyline
And then the Americans saw the sign,
The two AWOL planes heading straight for the American's pride.

In seconds the two planes hit,
It was shocking, it made some people sick,
Steel churning, people burning on the day that shocked the world,
People dying in the carnage.

By 5 o'clock it was all over the news,
The building was reduced to ash,
No one knew who'd done it, there were no clues,
What a sad day, Americans will pray.

We will not forget that sad day,
Where many Americans faded away,
But the spirit of New York carries on,
Even though the people of 9/11 have gone.

Daniel Bates (12)
Burscough Priory Science College

Young Monsters

Young, little monsters that play baseball at night,
Who hit a home run in the night,
On the third strike, you're out for the night.

Under the covers at night,
The bogeyman man comes to give you a fright.
Now that it is midnight, it is time to fight,
The Demon Headmaster's killer kite.

Now that it is morning, it is time to get dressed and behave,
Because if you don't,
You will be the Demon Headmaster's slave.

At lunchtime we have food fights every time
Until the Demon Headmaster says,
But the only day we don't, is Friday,
Because it is time to behave,
So that you can go home for the day
After lunchtime on a Friday.

Jamall Thomason (12)
Burscough Priory Science College

In Hiding

Anne Frank wrote a diary to stop confusion,
While hiding away to avoid persecution,
Anne's religion faded,
Amsterdam was invaded,
The family were in danger again.

'Who has inflicted this upon us?' she said,
Nothing to do but lie awake in bed,
Her thoughts were all that she had left,
Except dear Kitty, her only friend,
The family were safe now.

Anne's dream, when older, was to be a writer,
Just to be famous,
But this war would not let her,
This is what she wrote . . .

'It is God that has made us as we are,
But it will be God, too, who will raise us up again.
If we bear all this suffering and if there are still Jews left,
When it is over, then Jews instead of being doomed, will be
held up as an example.'

Sara Baldwin (13)
Burscough Priory Science College

The London Bombings

It all began as a normal day in London,
But then there was a *bang,*
Followed by a *clang,*
The train was demolished,
As well as the Underground being polished.

People died, it was a horror,
But what they didn't know,
There was going to be another,
One on a bus, it was a suicide bomber,
People saw him but didn't stop him.

There was another, another on a train,
It caused a lot of pain,
It was a horrific attack,
Similar to the ones in Iraq.

There was another, why?
It was on a train, why do you do this?
What do you gain?
There was a try,
Stupid people getting ready for others to die,
It all ended, there was no more.

Luke Kelly (12)
Burscough Priory Science College

My Army

My army was sometimes big and sometimes small
But one day we took one great fall
Because we had one problem
Our army was something big and sometimes small.

Green we were not, not blue, but green
Our emblem was small
But our army was sometimes big and sometimes small
That's what it was, big and small.

Blue, we are, not red, not green
Because our army is very tall
And definitely not big and small.

Blue we were, but our army was big and small
And definitely not tall
Green we are and still the army is big and small
And always will be big and small.

Lewis Matthews (12)
Burscough Priory Science College

Charlie's Family Starves

Snowy winter's day
In the snow they play
Each day all they had
Were three measly meals, it was sad.

Mr Bucket's job went bust
So there were only crusts
For the family to eat
There wasn't even any meat.

Charlie's tummy was rumbling, it wouldn't stop!
Then he found fifty pence on the ground.
He went to the nearest shop,
There he bought some chocolate.

Charlie ate his chocolate,
He took the change home to his mum.
His mum was very happy,
She then went to get food for the family.

Jenny Moss (12)
Burscough Priory Science College

Hurricane Katrina

Electricity lost, power cables ripped down
Families fleeing out of town.
People prayed
For God's aid.
Oh destructive Katrina.

Cars flying in the air
People watching, waiting in despair.
Winds still strong enough to rip off roofs
Tear down trees,
As Hurricane Katrina fled over the seas.
The mighty Katrina.

People to the left of them
People to the right of them
People behind them
Bashed and battered.
Plunged into the wind of a storm,
Taken back to where they were born.
The violent Katrina.

People fled from their homes
As Hurricane Katrina left nothing but rotting bones.
We were just waiting for the winds to die
As the clouds closed, there was no blue sky.
The deadly Katrina.

Michael Jones (13)
Burscough Priory Science College

Buried Alive

16th August 2005
The day our dear daughter was buried alive.
Playing in the sand with her brother Joe
The tragedy to come, we were yet to know.

Abbie was a girl always full of fun
Laughing and splashing that day in the sun.
Our two happy children were soon to become one.

Little did we know how that day would end,
Our broken hearts will never mend.

16th August 2005
The day our dear Abbie was buried alive.
The hole was deep, but she had no fear,
Knowing Mum, Dad and Joe were always near.

Silently, soundlessly, swiftly, the hole fell in,
Burying our Abbie deep within.
We tried to pull her out,
Emergency services arrived without a shout.

'Soft sand, beautiful sand,' the brochure said,
Perhaps it was, but now Abbie is dead.
16th August 2005
The day our dear daughter died.

Amy Wells (13)
Burscough Priory Science College

The Motorbike Crash

Speeding on at the Championship League race,
Roaring past, with hair in his face,
He swooped round the corner with lots of pace,
For all that had happened, he had left no trace.

He came round the corner with lots of speed
And came off his bike in a ragging lead,
Despite what had happened he lay there in need
And pleaded for a place in the Champion's League.

They raced him to hospital to get him some help,
With a nasty breakage he began to yelp,
He hardly thought about his great fame,
But was still in surgery in great pain.

He was back on his feet in no time at all,
But will always remember the day he had his great fall,
Despite what had happened, he still had a great face,
But will always remember the Championship race.

Natalie Pickering (12)
Burscough Priory Science College

Hallowe'en

H allowe'en was soon to be
A s Shane and Walker made a plan
L et's give Tabby and Lee a scare
L ee and Tabby will run a mile
O ur plan will make us happy
W e live to scare
E ach of us will get our revenge
E very year we will give an ultimate scare
N ever scare us without our revenge.

Jordan Weston (12)
Burscough Priory Science College

Hurricane Rita

Industrial town of 56,000
America's fourth largest city.
US history's largest evacuation,
More than two million flee northwards.
Hours of lasting traffic jams,
Petrol stations run out.

Protected Port Arthur,
By 17ft levees.
At least that's what they thought,
A 25ft storm surge was predicted to commence.
Prayers made for the city's fate,
Say a prayer for Texas.

Convoys of fire engines and police,
Pulled out at noon.
Last to leave the coastal city,
Warnings stretched 450 miles wide.
Along the coast,
Be calm, stay strong,
Say a prayer for Texas.

The monster hurricane,
Thunders ashore.
Three inches a minute,
Of substantial rain,
140mph winds.
6000 homes destroyed,
16,000 left homeless,
$8billion of damage,
Be calm, stay strong.

Jonathan Hall (12)
Burscough Priory Science College

London Bombs

On the 21st July,
Suddenly all went bad.
They couldn't stop them,
The bombs went mad.
Just this one place it all went down,
The little train station,
In the middle of the town.

The police started searching,
They searched left and right.
Will they find them?
Well, they might.
People charging here and there,
There was no time to stop and stare.

'It's just not fair,'
The people said.
'We loved the ones,
Who now are dead.'
How can such evil here be done?
The kind of war which can't be won.

Days have passed,
Nothing was found.
It was not safe to live
In London Town.
But life goes on,
It's sad but true,
Just left with memories of the ones we knew.

Megan Elloy (12)
Burscough Priory Science College

Katrina's Wrath

People running,
There was no space to breathe,
The hurricane hit,
As they started to leave,
Winds rose high,
Waters flooded,
Death was night,
The city was gutted!

Oh, Hurricane Katrina,
You are so wild,
As deadly as a bomb,
Our city was defiled,
Oh, Hurricane Katrina,
You left such destruction,
With floods and winds,
You left us in terrible condition!

Bush, where were you?
What took so long?
Crying and screaming,
We sat there waiting,
Hoping and praying,
Praying to be saved!

When all that was left was the dead,
New Orleans, the ghost city,
More than 42,000 had left,
Fled from the city of hell!

Shanice Kay (12)
Burscough Priory Science College

Guerrilla Fighters

Guerrilla fighters were very sneaky people,
They could kill people without others knowing,
They use guns that do not make a lot of noise,
So the guns don't alert the enemy that they are there.

They can kill with their bare hands and operate
Deep behind enemy lines,
In trenches, bushes . . . even pines!
When they go through the jungle they make lethal traps,
You've got to be careful you don't have a mishap!

They use knives and garrotes and only work in small teams,
That way they don't get seen!
The weapons they use are riffles and M1 grenades,
They shoot them with their deadly hands!

Andrew Rimmer (12)
Burscough Priory Science College

Katrina

Katrina her name
At high speed she came
Loud noises she made
Making people afraid.

Thrashing and crashing
Spinning and swirling
Shouting and screaming
As the people are fleeing.

Destroying and flooding
Rushing and gushing
Big messes she made
People afraid.

Neck deep in water
The disease spread faster
With supplies now here
Katrina's long gone.

Megan Kate Walls (12)
Burscough Priory Science College

Disaster, Rita Strikes Again!

Hurricane Rita
I wouldn't want to meet her
She crashed through the town
And made a hole in the ground
Hurricane Rita, I wouldn't want to meet her.

People fled the storm
With only memories of their homes
They were horrified by what they had seen
Because she had wiped the streets clean
Hurricane Rita, I wouldn't want to meet her.

They cried in distress
For the loved ones they had left
Now that she has gone
The people have to soldier on
Hurricane Rita, I'm glad I didn't meet her.

Ryan Jennings (12)
Burscough Priory Science College

Christmas For The Homeless

There are 380,000 people who have no home
380,000 people who are all alone.

Why does this happen?
What have they done?
Have they done something bad to get what they have?
Stop, stop, this has made me so sad.

But then 3,500 people
Who are brave and strong
Came to help at Christmas
To make it long and fun!

When it's Christmas and you're having fun
Think of all the homeless that are all alone.

Theo Serkumian (12)
Burscough Priory Science College

The Reds

While all the world is watching,
On this Champions' day,
We, the Reds, feel extremely proud,
Fans in their hundreds shout as we play.

Whistle blows . . . we take first shot,
Nerves of steel, we build our hopes,
Adrenaline kicks in,
We will win!

Half-time arrives,
3-0 down,
Benitez is cross,
He ticks us off,
This gives us power,
We score and score and score!

Penalties arrive, they are a must,
The final score is ours,
Liverpool is coming home,
AC Milan, there's no beating us,
We're the Champions once more!

Hannah Hall (12)
Burscough Priory Science College

Mean Girls

Cady's with the mean girls,
So she has to be curls and pearls,
She realises she's gotta be cool,
But maths isn't the mean girls' rule.

Regina is the plastic queen,
Though she's pretty, she is so mean,
She's trying to spoil things for Cady,
So she's nota very nice lady.

Gretchen's Regina's puppy-dog,
She hangs onto her like a log,
She'll do anything for her,
Anyone's feelings! She doesn't care.

Karen is so ultra dumb,
She doesn't know her finger from her thumb,
She can't even catch a ball,
I doubt she can make a telephone call.

Then it ended one fine day,
They all went a different way.

Becky Power (12)
Burscough Priory Science College

Teenage Troubles

You don't understand us,
You don't even care,
You're too busy nagging us,
But parents, beware!

We feel very angry,
We feel very down,
We walk around school
Wearing a frown.

All the things you say to us,
Make no sense at all,
You might as well stand there,
Talking to the wall!

I'm not interested in you,
Or the things you say,
It's all rubbish in my head,
So just go away!

Natalie Cheetham (12)
Burscough Priory Science College

Survival

Billy's situation was terrifying
He knew his best chance of survival
Was to stay in the yacht
And wait, wait to be rescued.

If he was going to be rescued,
He knew it would take at least two days
For a boat or helicopter to arrive
Waiting, waiting to be rescued.

He only just had his head above water,
The air in the hull was limited by the
Presence of so much water,
Wait, wait, waiting to be rescued.

He knew he was in big danger,
The supply of oxygen was running out fast
Wait, wait, wait, waiting to be rescued.

Will he be rescued?

Phil Gibbs (12)
Burscough Priory Science College

The Match Of Dreams

Manchester and Munich, the match it was
The European Cup, the reward it was
They were ready, the whistle blew
The match had begun, the match of dreams.

The crowd were singing, both sides were drawn
Until quite soon, when Munich attacked
They ran and ran, they huffed and puffed
When eventually it came, the goal they had dreamed

It was the 90th minute, Manchester were doomed
The journey for nothing, Munich were amazed
Four added minutes, enough for a goal.

In the 91st minute, Manchester took a corner
It swung in the box, when from out of nowhere
Came Sheringham's head
The ball went in, Manchester went mad.

The match was drawn at 93 minutes
But another corner was awarded
Into the box, the ball drove in
Cole was there his foot stuck out
Manchester had scored in the dying moments
Munich were down, down on the floor
The whistle blew, the match was won.

Callum Spencer (12)
Burscough Priory Science College

Oil In The Sea

As her engines fell asleep,
The water started to seep.
The tide pushing and bullying,
Her into the shallows,
The crew cried,
Man the life boats,
Man the life boats.

The crew crushed,
As the tide pushed.
The ship started to bleed,
Oil spilling everywhere,
The animals swimming anywhere,
In panic of the black.

Oil lapping against the rocks,
As birds flew away in flocks.
Crabs and starfish covered in oil,
As the engines in the ship started to boil.

But then the sun started to appear,
The NSPCA hope was here.
The fish could swim again
And the crabs were free,
The seals were happy
And so were we.

Adam Feeney (13)
Burscough Priory Science College

A Summer's Day

I went for a walk one summer's day,
But it took me an unusual way.
I saw trees that whistled in the breeze
And quiet rivers that flowed with ease.

I saw creatures rustling in the leaves,
And birds chirping in the trees.
I saw ramblers walking along the paths
And ducks taking their evening baths.

I saw fish racing up the stream
And waterfalls like in a dream.
I saw leaves falling to the ground
And I thought, *what a peaceful sound.*

I saw clouds racing across the sky,
As I watched the birds fly by.
I saw people moving from place to place
And it felt like I was in a race.

As the sun began to set,
I decided to head home before it got wet
And all the things I saw that day,
Were magical in every way.

Nina Lee (13)
Burscough Priory Science College

The Ghost I Saw

There she was at the table,
She died because of the cable,
She didn't read the label,
There she was at the table.

With her pearl ring,
She started to sing,
I tried to run,
But she shot me with a gun.

There I was on the ground,
I couldn't even make a sound,
She put her foot on my head,
I really thought I was dead.

My body went numb,
I couldn't feel my thumb,
I was going pale and gold,
I could see the ring shine gold.

I thought this was the end of me,
But then my nan came in to see,
Then woke me out of my dream,
Soon I was watching my favourite team.

Jack Winrow (12)
Burscough Priory Science College

A Hero In A Hospital Bed

Arthur Penhaligon waiting in a hospital bed
Stomach churning with such dread.
Master of the lower house, master of the far reaches
Heir to the house and of all the creatures.

Then he heard something like a train
Out of the wall came something that would cause pain.
Then, out of nowhere, came a boat on sea,
With sails as green as a chestnut tree.

There he was, a boy on a steel bed,
Soon thinking that he will be dead.
Was the boat going to pick him up,
Or had he finally ran out of luck?
The boat stopped on its side
Majestically floating on the tide.
Ropes came down to climb onto the ship,
But instead it wrapped around the bed.

The bed was stolen from the boy, he was frustrated
Like it had stolen its favourite toy.
He plunged into the sea below
The ship was gone, could it be so?
So he swam as fast as he could, to find land, he surely would
And finally a glimmer of luck, he found a buoy all covered in muck
He climbed on it, exhausted and hurting his head
And strangely his hand went red.
He was relieved about the buoy that saved his soul,
His only quest was to meet his goal.

Jefferson Bond (12)
Burscough Priory Science College

Best Friends

Alice and Gemma were born together,
They go to the same school.
Live round the corner
And in very hot weather,
Love to play in their pool,
But they've been best friends forever.

When they were 11 years old,
Alice moved to Scotland, which is cold.
Gemma didn't want her to leave,
So she kept saying, 'Please!'
So they ran away,
For just one day,
Although their dream was dead, when they were found together,
But they've been best friends forever.

Alice had been gone for ages and Gemma was sad,
She was so mad,
So she asked to go to Scotland,
Although she was kicked out when she got there,
But they've been best friends forever.

Months later it was their birthday,
They woke up together,
To find a big present,
Which they'd sent each other through the post,
But they've been best friends forever.

Katie Waring (12)
Burscough Priory Science College

Abuse Is Wrong

National Society for the Prevention of Cruelty to Children,
Your sister, your brother, your child, your grandchildren,
What would you do if it happened to you?
Do you know someone who it might have happened to?
What would you do if it happened to you?

You were unsure if abuse was taking place,
Not knowing the right thing to do,
Not knowing what would happen next,
Not knowing the safety for the child,
But what if it happened to you?

Give advice when asked,
Let the abuser be unmasked,
You'd feel your life was at an end,
The abuse may be non-stop,
What if the child was yours?
What would you do if it happened to you?

You know bullying is wrong,
You know your life should be long,
Cutting it short would be a waste,
Don't let the abuser be replaced,
Get rid of this person,
Let their sins do them well,
Let the child have their life,
The child inside is dying,
What would you do if the child really died?

Lisa Sutton (12)
Burscough Priory Science College

The Great Sabre-Toothed Tiger Battle

Sabre-toothed tigers all around,
Creeping gently without a sound.
Getting ready for the hunt,
The sabre-toothed tigers stood at the front.

Loading down groups of men,
The enemies hid in their den.
Setting up camp all around,
The bad men stood without a sound.

All in position the tigers glared,
Looking wonderfully as they stared.
Imagining meat,
The tigers prepared their feet.

Prepared to fight all the men,
Everyone came out of the den.
Firing bullets through the jungle,
All the bullets in a bundle.

All tigers sound the attack,
Being shot at in the back.
Pouncing on men the tigers did,
Most men feeling the people hid.

The battle was over, the tigers had won,
Not one man standing with a gun.
'Back to the jungle,' a tiger said,
So all the tigers went to bed.

Alan Mawdsley (12)
Burscough Priory Science College

The Pride Of Britain

The World Cup qualifiers are here,
England are the favourites,
But Wales should not fear,
England are world class,
But it's hard to stop Wales,
In top gear.

The whistle blows,
For the start,
Everyone knows they'll
Play one hundred percent heart,
It's been forty-five minutes now
And they have already proven
They're not tarts.

It's the second half
And Joe Cole has just scored
And the England crowd roared,
England haven't played well,
But neither has Wales.

The final whistle blows
And all the fans go,
As all the Wales' fans hide,
The England fans sing with pride.

Andrew Kenyon (13)
Burscough Priory Science College

The Unfortunate Plane Crash

It was the day of the holiday,
When they pulled onto the runway,
Spirits were high,
Nobody had a clue they were going to die.

The plane climbed to 10,000 feet,
When the passengers felt a shudder in their seat,
They began to panic and cry,
Everyone thought the y were going to die.

It was the power the plane lacked,
Because a fan blade had cracked,
The diagnosis was bad,
The crew was very sad.

Drastic action was taken,
The pilot's decision was mistaken,
The wrong engine was stopped,
Oh, how the plane dropped.

The plane crashed onto the M1,
All hopes were gone,
At 2.24
There were deaths galore.

At 125 miles per hour,
It all went sour,
900 metres from
The control tower.

Mike Edwards (12)
Burscough Priory Science College

Four Seasons

When winter comes,
Snow and ice,
Makes the scenery very nice,
With snowmen and snowballs
And thick layers of snow so tall.

When spring comes,
Plants and flowers begin to peep,
Awakening from there long sleep,
Birds and butterflies flutter by,
In the beautiful dark blue sky.

When summer comes,
Children play and have some fun,
In the beautiful yellow sun,
The smell of grass on a summer's day
And a field of corn and a field of hay.

When autumn comes,
Leaves fall to the ground,
They turn red, yellow and a nice shade of brown,
Then along comes the wind and rain
And so the cycle goes round again.

Tom Malone (12)
Burscough Priory Science College

The Living Dummy

Kate and Amanda were messing around
And found a slip of paper
That brought the dummy to life,
Frightened as they were to tell,
I grabbed Slappy and threw him on the floor
And whacked his head on the wall,
I searched for the slip of paper,
Not there, not there, not there.

I was breathing hard, heart pounding like a ball bouncing,
Staring at his mouth hanging open,
As if he was going to laugh,
Sweat dripping from my face,
Food all over the walls,
On the floorboards, so messy,
Kate trembling, Amanda crying.

Screaming, screaming, screaming,
Dining room a real mess,
Slappy covered in sauce,
Squealing like a little mouse,
Squirming, trying to escape,
Kate and Amanda held him back.

Tasha Harrison (12)
Burscough Priory Science College

Battle Under Farthen Dur

In the mountains of Farthen Dur,
There is an almighty war.
With the evil Urgals near,
The dwarves are now hiding in fear.
The Urgal feet sound *scritch, scritch,*
Then dwarves pour out the burning pitch.
Two more battalions moving in,
The dwarves now wondering, *can we win?'*

The dragon's fury makes it roar,
But the Urgals keep coming more and more.
The dwarf king's wrath is passed around,
As even more Urgals hit the ground.
Hrothgar is the dwarven king
And gives his axe a mighty swing.
Whilst protecting his loyal guards,
He hurls a spear twenty yards.

Whilst holding the flood of Urgals back,
They fire arrows coloured black.
With the dragon's armour crushed,
Faster and faster the Urgals rushed.
With Eragon stuck at the top of the stairs,
The Urgals are marching through in pairs.
With the Urgal advance not slowing down,
The dwarves are scared of losing their crown.

Wearing black armour, he is here,
The evil Shade is coming near.
As he walks through the great halls,
He blasts past the standing walls.
Until he finds a worthy fight,
He just shows off his deadly might.
Then all of a sudden he is slain,
And Farthen Dur is safe again.

Christopher Rice (12)
Burscough Priory Science College

Car Crash

Looking and watching the stars
Looking up to see Mars
All of the stars are twinkling in the sky
I was to only wonder why
Was it a special night?
I had no idea.

The car started to speed up
So I stopped looking out of the window
And drifted in and out of sleep
Listening to the music beat.

The car shuddered and went out of control
And suddenly onto the other side
I stared and cried
I closed my eyes
I see the size
Of the lorry coming towards us.

I tried to put my seatbelt on, but it was too late
Everything went blank
A big thud on my head
I heard glass shatter everywhere
I didn't know what to do or dare.

I didn't know what to say as all my feelings went away
But I still heard the people say
Everyone screaming, shouting me
My bones smashed up into pieces
I hit the floor
And all my life was no more
But those people that were shouting me, had seatbelts on
And I was the only one who was stupid enough not to
And now I know why those stars twinkled so
I knew it was time to go.

Sian Lloyd (12)
Burscough Priory Science College

The Twin Towers

The Twin Towers stood in New York
One at 1362 feet high and the other at 1368
Both at 110 stories high
10 million square feet of flats and offices
This took seven years to build
At a cost of $1.5 billion dollars.

September 11th
An ordinary day
Ordinary lives
People came out of flats and into offices
Not knowing what was about to happen.

Then it happened
The first plane crashed into the first tower
The second crashed into the second tower
A terrible disaster
A terrible day.

September 11th
A day to remember
Not an ordinary day
No more ordinary lives
This day will always stay in our minds.

Rebecca Finch (12)
Burscough Priory Science College

College Student Frankie Smith

College student Frankie Smith
Was walking home from his midnight shift
He was working at a pizza place,
You really should have seen his face,
Walking back to his own place.

He heard a wailing from the bins
And it wasn't clanking tins,
Was it a cat?
Was it a dog?
Or it could be a frog.

He walked over to the bins,
There was no cat or dog,
Mr Smith got quite a shock,
For in the bins, very strangely,
Was a tiny, little wailing baby.

The tiny baby quite alive,
Was very lucky to survive,
With big brown eyes and lots of hair,
Very happily lying there,
With college student, Frankie Smith.

Molly Scott (12)
Burscough Priory Science College

Home

Home is where my mum and dad are,
Home is where my brother is,
Home is Comet (he's my dog),
Home is everything I love.

Home is where I laugh and play,
Home is where I spend all day,
Home is happy, home's not sad,
Home is good, but never bad.

Home's one place I don't need friends,
Even when the laughter ends,
Home's one place I can be on my own,
But even then, I'm never alone.

Home is jolly, not just a home,
Stuck to another, but not a bother,
Home's not grand, or rich, or big,
But it's where I love to live.

Home is perfect, not one thing wrong,
In my mind, I sing this song,
Home is safe, as safe as can be,
Home means all the world to me.

Erica Summers (12)
Burscough Priory Science College

The Race

Running fast,
All of the fences past.
You do not know what is at stake,
Or what kind of hero you may be
Your only wish is to leave the others
Hiding in your wake.

As your hooves pound out a rhythmic beat
The crowd jumps to its feet.
You summon your courage, strength and endurance
You are running to win!
But the race isn't over,
You have not won yet.

You would run forever,
If you had the chance.
Your rider and you together as one;
As you get closer and closer to winning the race,
Behind you is an ever-growing space.

You pass the line with flying colours,
But you must look behind to see the others
As they gave it their best try!
To the circle you go, to celebrate your win!

Jasmine Jones (12)
Burscough Priory Science College

The Big Bang

One normal day in London
People were just on the double-decker
On their way to somewhere nice
It was the 7th of July and very hot.

But then, all of a sudden, *bang!*
A big explosion on the double-decker bus
The bus was on fire
Oh no, what could have been put under the bus?

At nearly the same time
There was a bomb on the trains
Big bang explosion
Oh no, the double-decker and trains
It was so unexpected that day.

That day 56 people died
700 people were injured
No one will forget that day
July the 7th, Thursday, 12.30pm.

Jemma Dobson (12)
Burscough Priory Science College

Hurricane Rita

In Beaumont, Texas, Hurricane Rita struck
The rescue team came in their truck
Car windscreens smashed, lost of pieces went into faces
The Hurricane damaged lost of places.

Breeze block walls wouldn't hold
Because they were too old
People looking like beans
Swirled around like a washing machine
Brown flood water, people had to run
When the water got into shoes
It felt like a ton
When it reached 140 miles per hour
It looked like a tower.

Samuel Fletcher (12)
Burscough Priory Science College

Sir Alex

Ferguson and Queiroz were heading for the sack,
With all the boos,
They had to lose,
But now they lead the pack.

Morten Gamst Pedersen got the critics going,
Ruud van Nistelrooy on the 85th minute shut them up,
As they beat Benfica 2-1,
In the Champions League Cup.

Ryan Giggs scored a fluky free kick,
It put them one up,
When Benfica scored the equaliser, it made Sir Alex sick,
In the 85th minute he recovered very quick.

Sir Alex's team are sixth in the Premiership,
One point above Arsenal,
Can Wayne and Ruud get them top,
Or will Sir Alex get the chop?

Dan Hurst (12)
Burscough Priory Science College

Voldermort

V iolent best describes a man like me
O ccult is where I roam free
L ord of the Underworld, this I am
D estructive to all, if I can
E vil to all is my middle name
R evolting is my personal aim
M urderer is what people think of me
O nslaught is what I cause to be
R ebellious is what I am
T errible and awful I make your brain go *bam!*

Geoffrey Prytherch (13)
Burscough Priory Science College

The Chimps Are Free

Off we went to Belfast Zoo,
Zebras, lions, tigers too.
But why the police all around,
Holding bananas above the ground?

Suddenly, we heard a clatter,
Then a very loud scatter.
Then a load of chimps ran,
Followed by a policeman!

'But how did the chimps escape?'
We asked the lady by the gate.
'Well it was that clever Phoebe,
She organised for her fellow escapees.'

She propped a log against the gate,
Ready for the great escape.
And after three, the chimps were away,
Running down the dual carriageway.

Oh, what fun we had at the zoo,
Zebras, lions, tigers too.
But the chimps I didn't see,
Cos the clever things had broken free!

Stephanie Woods (13)
Burscough Priory Science College

Michael Owen Going To Newcastle And Getting His First Game

Michael Owen is a footballer and Newcastle is his club
He's signed a new contract with them and now he's playing good.
He's met all his teammates and the manager too.

He went to the football ground, St James' Park it's called
The supporters were there to meet him and were shouting his name
He went in the changing room to get his locker and peg
He sat next to Alan Shearer who is the captain of the club.

The team was ready for the match
Onto the pitch they went
All the crowd were chanting his name
The game had just started, the crowd began to roar.

Shearer scored the first goal to lots of applause
Michael Owen got the ball and dribbled past their players
He shot the ball into the goal and everyone cheered
The whistle blew, the game was over, Michael was a hero.

Charlotte Ross (12)
Burscough Priory Science College

The Troubles Of Timothy

Her poor son when he fell ill,
She stumbled through the woods,
To find a house to retrieve a pill.

As she arrived no one was in,
She sat on the step for him to arrive,
Just so her son could stay alive.

When he came back she ran to his door,
She even begged on the floor,
'My poor Timothy is ill.'
'We can't help him, I'll need to make a pill.'

As she was given three sachets,
She ran and ran back through the woods in a daze,
She gave him one a day,
By the third, he was okay.

Robert Rimmer (12)
Burscough Priory Science College

The Bombs That Hurt So Many

It was 7/7 on a summer's morning,
When tragedy struck with no warning,
Four explosions rocked the city
And left the country filled with pity,
Three trains and one bus were ripped apart,
Leaving people with a broken heart,
Emergency services rushing to help,
Crying people were letting out yelps,
56 people in the explosions died,
700 were injured but luckily survived,
There were four more bombs two weeks later,
However, this time it was only the detonator,
No one was hurt from this failed attack,
Only the memories of two weeks back,
Only the memories of two weeks back.

Jessica Fay (12)
Burscough Priory Science College

Raving Rita!

Is it possible?
Could it be?
Surely the destruction, you can already see.
Go west to Texas, New Orleans, hope,
If this thing was to hit them, how would they cope?

Their hopes were shattered with a great big bang!
As rain and winds crashed and clanged.
Trees thrown across roads, blocking the way,
For the residents of New Orleans, it was looking grey.

People's homes and lives were put at risk,
Because of the killer winds that blew so brisk.
Mud-brown water and gushing floods,
Running through the city, scattering goods.

Twice in a month, Mother Nature had struck,
Oh, how many people's lives she took.
Many people's lives were taken that day,
Just because they stood in Rita's way!

Hannah Murphy (12)
Burscough Priory Science College

Growing Up

When I was one I could recognise a swan
When I was two I could tie my shoe,
When I was three I was stung by a bee,
When I was four I could open the door,
When I turned five I could do the jive,
When I was six I could stir and mix,
When I was seven I learned about Heaven,
When I turned eight I learned how to skate,
When I turned nine I made a wind chime,
When at last I was ten I made a chicken pen.

Kelly Seddon (12)
Burscough Priory Science College

Where Would We Be Without Technology?

Where would we be
Without technology?
There'd be no computers
And we wouldn't be commuters
On the train,
Or on the plane.
The hospitals would go insane.

But then again . . .
No guns, no bombs,
No nuclear wars.
Iraq wouldn't be devastated
And things here wouldn't be complicated
So where would we be
Without technology?

What would we be
Without technology?
No games consoles to play on
No shuttles on the moon
And everyone would be a buffoon
Without a calculator.

But then again . . .
We wouldn't be slaves
To computers or games
And we wouldn't be overweight
So, what would we be
Without technology?

Dominic Spencer (13)
Burscough Priory Science College

The Strongest Boy

The name that people give him
Would not just frighten bees,
It isn't as soft as Tinkerbell
But as fierce as Hercules.

This boy is just eleven,
Been training since he was two,
He's learnt to do the splits
And never wears a single shoe.

Can lift three times his body weight
And not break into a single sweat,
His mum and dad might look after him,
But they treat him as a pet.

His first name is Richard,
His last name is Sandrak,
He might look big and strong,
But really is as soft as flapjack.

He may be just a boy,
But has muscles like a man,
He might be just eleven,
But can do anything a man can.

This might be supernatural,
But really it's not a dream,
He does not eat much chocolate,
Nor vanilla ice cream.

Billy Bimpson (12)
Burscough Priory Science College

Hurricanes Are Terrible Things

Hurricanes are terrible things,
They are a sound which make your ears ring,
Swirling around like they've got wings,
Hurricanes are terrible things.

Hurricanes ripping of rooves,
Move around making violent moves,
They are anything but smooth,
Hurricanes are terrible things.

They can spark into a fifteen foot surge,
Like the click of fingers they can emerge,
They are not to be encouraged,
Hurricanes are terrible things.

When they have gone it's like a hundred giants have been,
There is nothing but wreckage to be seen,
They smash and batter which is mean,
Hurricanes are terrible things.

James Ross (12)
Burscough Priory Science College

Mrs Frisby And The Cat

Mrs Frisby went straight out the tunnel,
The sun glows as bright as fire,
Day after day it gets higher and even higher.

The cat is like a fireball,
If it spots you a mile away it will be on you in five seconds flat,
The cat has got very good eyesight,
The only thing the cat cannot do is get down a hole.

Mrs Frisby is so scared when she exits her home,
Well, why doesn't she stay in then?
Well, because she must keep her family alive,
Especially her son, Timothy,
But she is always quiet, but ever so scared.

Mrs Frisby always gets past the cat safely,
But many do not.
Luckily enough, Mrs Frisby gets past safely
And the cat does not see her.

Bethany Seddon (12)
Burscough Priory Science College

Donkey Days

Cheeky! Cheeky donkey!
Learning how to open bolted stable doors,
She steals the feed, for her need,
She isn't always happy with grazing on grassy moors.

A dab hand people say,
Kicking locks and sliding bolts,
Using her teeth won't make her jolt.

To complete her opening operation,
She rests her head on the door,
Action stations,
Now she walks backwards and then . . .
She's in!

Her final task is pinching food,
From her hungry companions,
The whole mission is done
And all for a bucket of food!

Amelia Hales (12)
Burscough Priory Science College

Ripping Rita

Hurricane Rita whirling by,
Flattened homes but no one did die.
Lots of wind and plenty of rain,
Caused people hurt and some pain.

Hurricane Rita whirling alone,
Plenty of wind that was very strong.
People screaming and crying out loud,
All you could hear was the screaming of the crowd.

Hurricane Rita whirling away,
But another one will be back some day.
Probably worse but maybe better,
Let's just hope it doesn't get wetter.

Hurricane Rita has whirled past,
Went at a speed that was very fast.
Ripped by Rita and could have died,
Lucky are the ones who survived.

Laura Upton (12)
Burscough Priory Science College

Stoke City Vs Wolverhampton Wanderers 24/09/05

Crowd chanting in eager awe,
Awaiting the players' appearance,
Then out from the tunnel came the mighty Reds,
Ready for a game of endurance.

The rivals were ready and the sun shone bright,
As the whistle blew, Stoke had the odds,
The Britannia Stadium was aloud with a roaring chant,
Wolverhampton watched and prayed to their gods.

Darel Russell of Stoke had the first effort of the game,
A harmless volley over the bar,
Soon after that, Dubbery struck,
Going wide by afar.

Just before the halfway mark,
The Wolves' Seol Ki-Hyun, curved a brilliant cross,
But Carl Cort headed wide,
'Wakey, wakey, Wanderers!' Stoke's crowd yelled after the loss.

Not for long, as Seol was through again,
Centring the ball with a curling kick,
Carl Cort was there, again,
Only to score so City couldn't take the mick.

Straight after the restart of the half,
Kenny Miller headed home from close range,
But still the home supporters chanted:
'Wakey, wakey Wanderers!' - There was no change.

Many supporters trotted off home in anger,
Before Wolves scored another with a super free kick,
3-0, oh dear, as more went home,
But Buxton got one back with a header off a flick,
3-1 to Wolves, not *too* bad I suppose.

Matthew Foster (12)
Burscough Priory Science College

Hurricane K And R

Hurricane Katrina hit so fast
Destroyed everything in its path
Screams and shouts all around
Children orphaned
Parents never to be found.

Flood waters rising
People dying
Horrible sounds
Horrific sights
People running with fright.

People looking for their families
Don't know if they're dead or alive
Families split apart by this horrific wind
Thousands of people living on nothing
But scraps and dirty water.

Clearing up when a threat arrived
Hurricane Rita took the people by surprise
People fled their broken-down homes
Running for their lives.

Hurricane Rita stronger than the last
But slowed down as it went past
Even so, the result was devastating
And people missing their loved ones.

No one will ever get over this living nightmare
Thousands of people lost their friends
And families because of this natural disaster.

Abigail Gillard (12)
Burscough Priory Science College

Buzzing Bees

Panic! Panic! Everywhere!
Wasps buzzing round and round,
Arms and legs covered with bees,
Lines and lines they were,
It's all the teacher sees.

Thousands and thousands,
Swarming in towards me,
Messing around with nests,
Kicking and disturbing,
'No wonder we've got these pests!'

Emergency! Emergency!
As the bees attacked,
More and more they came,
Nearer and nearer they got,
'Will we ever be the same?'

'Safety, safety!'
Called the school teacher,
'Get in! Get in!'
'Slam the doors shut!'
Wasps are now swarming in!

Hannah Jackson (12)
Burscough Priory Science College

Tsunami

The earthquake was huge,
Three minutes it lasted.
The sea, how it blasted
And killed the 300,000.
At midnight it struck
And all the lives it took.
The place is now a dead town.

The ground, how it swayed,
The panic it made.
Destroying buildings, houses and flats.
People pulling dead bodies,
Out of the ground.
It wasn't pleasant,
The people, they drowned.

After three minutes,
The waves stopped.
Everyone was in dumb shock.
A dead town, a dead town,
That's all that it was,
When the terrible tsunami,
Hit them all with shock.

Tyree Rawsthorne (12)
Burscough Priory Science College

Hurricane Katrina

Katrina, Katrina, ruining your home,
Katrina, Katrina, quick get in the dome.
Hear it banging at the walls,
Hear the worried victims' calls.

See the flooding in the street,
The dead and dying at your feet.
I am here alive and well,
I hope my family are as well.

I cannot see them anywhere,
This whole place is in despair.
People are crying all around,
All you can hear is the dreaded sound.

In the dome it feels like hell,
The people in here can't be well.
No food, no drink, we may well die,
Yet I'm standing tall and refuse to cry.

As I step outside the dome,
I see no longer house or home.
All I see is horror and pain,
Surely this cannot ever happen again.

I see people in the street,
Yet they're not walking on their feet.
They float face up for all to see,
The result of this catastrophe.

Amanda Lawes (12)
Burscough Priory Science College

Mass Exodus

Millions flee as Rita roars in,
Many homes are going to go into the bin,
Chaos all around,
One-way traffic jams.
Here she comes,
Here she comes.

There's nothing we can do,
But to rebuild Texas anew,
A frightening nightmare,
Why the world would care,
Here she comes,
Here she comes.

A crashing curse storms through the street,
125mph winds it would meet,
Ripping rooftops off as she goes,
Frustration and anger flows, flows, flows,
There she goes,
There she goes.

Now she's gone,
After 16 hours of hell,
95% of Texans,
Had coped so well,
It will never be the same!
It will never be the same!

Eleanor Crewe (12)
Burscough Priory Science College

Jessie

Jessie, the luckiest dog around
Gets hurt whenever she touches the ground
Abandoned as a pup
No bigger than a cup
Jessie, the unluckiest dog around.

Started life at the airport,
No one to love and care for
When the Hides bought her
They had found Jessie, the luckiest dog around.

Plummeted down a cliff 30ft
Walked away without a cut
Bitten by a snake in Devon
Survived going to doggy Heaven
Jessie, the luckiest dog around.

Last gored by a stag
Surely her white flag
Too weak to make a sound
But still was found
Jessie, the luckiest dog around.

Tom Sheffield (12)
Burscough Priory Science College

Hurricane Katrina

Hurricane Katrina's devastation,
The horrific event that shocked the nation.
Hundreds dead and more to come,
Heaving and grieving for everyone.

Wind and rain that shattered glass,
But surely now she was soon to pass.
Death and flooding everywhere,
The horrible smell of disease and despair.

As she passed her strength was clear,
Nothing but silence they could hear.
Houses torn and ripped apart,
The clearing process was soon to start.

Clearing up was hard to take,
Much more was needed than a spade or a rake.
Power down and trees falling,
USA can you hear them calling?

Days passed till help was there,
Many people full of despair.
A lucky escape for the Gulf Bay,
Yet none knew what was on its way.

Joel Louttit (13)
Burscough Priory Science College

ABC Girls

A is for Amy
Maybe she wants a theme
For her birthday team.
She had pizza on the menu,
But Amy's was the venue.

B is for Bella
They went swimming as the main bit,
Lets just hope they all remember their kit.
When it was morning they all went home,
Not even touching their hair with a comb.

C is for Chloe
Cruelty is the word,
If you haven't already heard,
Daisy wasn't invited to sleep,
But that didn't go cheap.
Daisy did go in the end,
But only to start a new trend,
Anchovies on pizza.

D is for Daisy
They played football outside,
Chloe said she scored a goal
She lied!
They slept in a tent, it was good fun
In the morning they got a piece of bacon and a bun.

E is Emily
She had food that everyone liked,
Even her baby brother had something to bite.
They played football at the park,
Emily's dad called them all little sparks.
In the morning they were sad, the last sleepover was over!

Sammy Robinson (12)
Burscough Priory Science College

The Lonely Old Lady

Unloved and so lonely,
Locked in her home,
The poor and old lady,
Felt cold and alone.
With nothing to eat,
There was no one to help her,
The little old lady,
Died all on her own.

Her new door had no letter box,
So she never got her money,
She couldn't buy her food,
Not even a jar of honey!
No one came to see her,
From her big family,
Were they all too busy
Or did they just not care?

I feel so hungry!
I feel so scared!
I am so alone!
I am too scared to pick up the phone.

Found dead at her home,
Lying all on her own,
Unloved and so lonely,
The little old lady,
Died all on her own.

Adele Souther (12)
Burscough Priory Science College

The Ashes

Australia played cricket,
But lost every wicket,
England had won for good!
They played with bats made of wood.
The Ashes were over
Australia bowled over.

England should be proud,
Their supporters were loud,
They were a terrific crowd,
They played at the Oval,
How lovely, how grateful we truly are.

England celebrated,
Not even Australia were frustrated,
The players got their awards
And the little urn was England's
Oh, how everyone's stomach churned,
England had learned,
They can beat Australia
Hopefully, the next Ashes won't be a failure.

The players went home,
The Ashes was over
All they can do now, is train.

Jamie Nolan (12)
Burscough Priory Science College

Michael Owen

Michael Owen went to Newcastle, he did, he did
Despite the despair of the Liverpool fans
He went to Newcastle, he did, he did
I'm his biggest fan and a true Liverpool supporter
I am, I am.

Michael Owen went to Newcastle, he did, he did
He would have more fans at Liverpool
He would have done, he would have done
But Rafa Benitez couldn't get the money
He couldn't, he couldn't.

Michael Owen went to Newcastle, he did, he did
He's one of the best football players
That scores goals for fun, he does, he does
He dances around defenders to score for his team
To score, to score.

Michael Owen went to Newcastle, he did, he did
He's crushed my dreams of him coming back to Liverpool
He's crushed them, he's crushed them
Maybe next year we will have the money
To buy him, to buy him.

Matthew Manuel (12)
Burscough Priory Science College

The Day New Orleans Died

I was strong but motionless,
A breeze made new and fresh.
Out of the dark, damp air,
I became evil and wanted to become a scare.

People saw me and started to flee,
I heard screaming and shouting as I picked up the sea.
Still hearing screaming and shouting I began to laugh,
I came onto land and they all saw my wrath.

I was too strong for the city to bear,
People were dying, I didn't care.
I sped to the west, leaving people in fear,
There, I would slowly disappear.

I left the city, gone of sound,
People being rescued and found,
All quiet and still,
Until . . .
Next time.

Sean Kelly (12)
Burscough Priory Science College

The Lion In The Kitchen

I went on holiday last week
And I stayed in a hotel lobby
But it really did reek
Of horses and dogs and a great big moggy
But it was just fine for me.

Then one day I came back from a walk
And everyone started to talk
And then I saw it standing there
With its claws and its teeth and its fine, bushy fur
A lion in the kitchen
Nibbling on the cook!

'Oh my God!'
I cried at once
I then crept and sadly trod
Upon a spatula, sad to say
The lion leaped and ran away
With the cook in his jaws
He bounced upon his giant paws!

I really miss the sad old cook
And I wonder what it's like there now
Come on
Let's go and take a look . . .

Hannah Murphy (12)
Burscough Priory Science College

Football

Some people don't get football,
They say it's really boring,
From Everton to Liverpool,
10,000 fans are roaring.

They say it's really boring,
But do they really know?
10,000 fans are roaring,
The numbers seem to grow.

But do they really know?
Chelsea are always winning,
The numbers seem to grow,
Now 10,000 fans are singing.

Chelsea are always winning,
From Everton to Liverpool,
Now 10,000 fans are singing,
Some people don't get football.

Peter Atkinson (12) & Jordan Armstrong (11)
Ingleton Middle School

Tadpoles

One is thin, one is fat,
They could be frogs,
Both are scared of the cat,
They don't like dogs.

They could be frogs,
All on their own,
They don't like dogs,
Now they have grown.

All on their own,
They're in the pond,
Now they have grown,
They have a special bond.

There in the pond,
They're scared of the cat,
They have a special bond,
One is thin, one is fat!

Becky Birnie (12) & Emilly Thane (11)
Ingleton Middle School

Christmas

Mum's in the kitchen making mince pies,
Dad's sat in his chair,
Flying round above Mum's head are those flippin' flies
Dad's being nothing but fair.

Dad's in his chair,
This morning we rushed down,
Dad's being nothing but fair,
This morning we found loads of éclairs.

This morning we rushed down,
The Christmas tree was gleaming,
This morning we found loads of éclairs,
Our faces all were beaming.

The Christmas tree is gleaming,
Flying round above Mum's head are those flippin' flies,
Our faces all are beaming,
Mum's in the kitchen making mince pies.

Bethan Harrison & Chloe Smethurst (11)
Ingleton Middle School

The Sky

It's bright and blue,
It has fluffy clouds,
It's always new,
The birds squawk loud.

It has fluffy clouds,
Planes fly by,
The birds squawk loud,
Up in the beautiful bright blue sky.

Planes fly by,
Nothing's ever tame,
Up in the beautiful bright blue sky,
Nothing stays the same.

Nothing's ever tame,
It has fluffy clouds,
Nothing stays the same,
The birds squawk loud.

Isobel Marshall (11)
Ingleton Middle School

Summer

Summer is sunny and warm,
We lick our ice lollies.
There is never a storm,
Children play with sand and dollies.

We lick our ice lollies,
Summer is never cold.
Children play with sand and dollies,
The colour of summer is bright and bold.

Summer is never cold,
Trees and flowers grow strong and tall.
The colour of summer is bright and bold,
We play on the beach with our ball.

Trees and flowers grow strong and tall,
There is never a storm.
We play on the beach with our ball,
Summer is sunny and warm.

Elsa Priestley (12) & Emma Taylor (11)
Ingleton Middle School

Children With No Happiness

They have no happiness without their families,
I have no hope for them,
I pray they will survive,
Knowing the world is full of viruses.

Their faces have no light,
Knowing the world is full of viruses,
They have no hope for themselves,
I have no hope for them.

Their faces have no light,
I wonder if they will be OK,
They have no hope for themselves,
They have no toys to play with.

I wonder if the will be OK,
They have no happiness without their families,
They have no toys to play with,
I pray they will survive.

Melanie Morphet (11)
Ingleton Middle School

Children With No Hope

I have no hope at all,
Living in a rough place,
I would dream to get a toy ball,
I would wish for a little space.

Living in a rough place,
People are so mean,
I would wish for a little space,
Anything to be clean.

People are so mean,
I wonder, why me?
Anything to be clean,
I would dream to be free.

I wonder, why me?
I would dream to get a toy ball,
I would dream to be free,
I have no hope at all.

Shauna Tennant (11)
Ingleton Middle School

What's Happening?

The terrible tsunami
The earthquake in Pakistan
Stop watching silly Toonami
There are dead people from Afghanistan.

The earthquake in Pakistan
The 11th of September
Dead people in Afghanistan
You have got to remember.

The 11th of September
The war in Iraq
You have to remember
People getting chucked away in sacks.

The terrible tsunami
The earthquake in Pakistan
Stop watching silly Toonami
There are dead people from Afghanistan.

Liam Ellershaw (11)
Ingleton Middle School

There Are Monsters In My Head

When my mum says, 'Right, go to bed,'
I always get scared,
I have monsters in my head,
The monsters I imagine look like gremlins, but long haired.

I always get scared,
My mum says there's no such thing,
The monsters I imagine look like gremlins, but long haired,
They also love to sing.

My mum says there's no such thing,
As I stay up all night,
They also love to sing,
I always get a fright.

As I stay up all night,
When my mum says, 'Right, go to bed,'
I always get a fright,
I have monsters in my head.

Hayley Mace & Joanne Cornthwaite (11)
Ingleton Middle School

Winter

My knees are in the snow,
The little stones of hail,
The temperature is low,
Hail on my cat's tail.

The little stones of hail,
Snowballs flying all about,
The temperature is low,
Snowmen roundabout.

Snowballs flying all about,
Frost on the fields,
Snowmen roundabout,
More frost far afield.

Frost on the fields,
Robins everywhere,
More frost far afield,
They could be anywhere.

Anne-Marie Townley (12)
Ingleton Middle School

Supernana!

Supernana has a cat
Supernana squashed it flat
Supernana ate the cat
Supernana spat it back.

Supernana squashed it flat
Supernana felt so fat
So Supernana spat it back
Supernana has a cat.

Adam Sherriff & James Michael Lund (11)
Ingleton Middle School

The Flood

The flood of New Orleans
All as wet as a fish
Nothing to eat but beans
With not so much as a dish.

All as wet as a fish
House reduced to twigs
Waiting to be rescued
Remember those who died.

House reduced to twigs
The government is as slow as a slug
Remember those who died
Freedom or death.

The government is as slow as a slug
Nothing to eat but beans
Freedom or death
The flood of New Orleans.

Robert Hinde (11)
Ingleton Middle School

Badgers

I'm out at night
Not in light
Making my bed
Digging ahead
Out searching
Can hear something lurching
Claws are out
Can see it about
Caught me in my act
Knows the facts
I'm after it now
It has no chance
It's supper!

Kayleigh Devine (11)
Lostock Hall Community High School & Arts College

As The Ball Of Fire Rises

As the ball of fire rises,
I feel my legs give way,
My body's being lifted high,
In the morning of the day.

Don't know where I'm going,
The sun is shining bright,
I'm lying on a bed of air,
Being blinded by the light.

A big, shiny diamond in the ground,
On it, children laughing and playing,
A rock solid lake made of water,
The children with joy are screaming.

The street lamps around me come on,
The bright sky is falling,
Children are now going to bed,
The stunning light is going.

We're being invaded by darkness,
Which has given the light its debts,
My eyes are closing all alone,
As the ball of fire sets.

Bethany Waring (12)
Lostock Hall Community High School & Arts College

Alien Poem

He was coloured blueish-grey
And had travelled a long way
Three long fingers and wide eyes
Tree stump head and ears like pies
He flies in the skies in his silver saucer
Came to Earth for a sample of water.

Tongue made of rock and teeth of ice
He is really so very nice
He plays football in outer space
And he loves a good race
Comes from the planet Dwight
Goes by the name of Billy Crite.

Joe Carthy (11)
Lostock Hall Community High School & Arts College

Why?

Why do we hunt between the trees?
Shooting birds beyond the leaves.
Wandering, wandering, the poor little mole,
Trying so hard to find his hole.

Why do we poach fluffy, little rabbits?
While they're busily doing their daily habits.
As hedgehogs go in their spiky balls,
So neat and tidy, very small.

Rabbits have pricked up ears,
Warning the animals, especially the deers.
The deer run, in such a fright,
As hunters look, throughout the night.

Alexandra Jackson (11)
Lostock Hall Community High School & Arts College

My Brother

I was the first born, loved and cherished,
I had everything I wanted, even a play shed.
I had a loving mum and loving dad,
Everything was good, nothing was bad.
I had my first birthday alone,
I liked everything for my own.
That was when they decided to create him,
Every single, evil limb.
Now I have to share every toy,
Why couldn't it be a girl, not a boy?
As I grew up,
He grew up.
Everything turned into a disaster,
Because he thinks he is the master.
Everything I got,
He copied the lot.
Eventually, I got something in my brain that sent me mad,
Which quiet often made my mum and dad sad.
I used to smash a thing or two,
Then my temper grew and grew.
Now I take a pill,
Two a day to help me chill.
By him I used to get bullied,
Then I felt as small as an arachnid.
Crouching away,
Trying to avoid him every day.
He used to call me things, like 'Stressy Bessy' or 'Stress Head',
I felt ignored like I was dead.
Now my insides boil and brew,
Every time I hear the dreadful name, Andrew.

Martin Carmon (13)
Lostock Hall Community High School & Arts College

Candid Camera

Off to Wales we went one day
Weather was good, *hip hip hooray*
Got to the beach and into the sea
Out comes Dad's camera, *hee, hee, hee*
We stand and smile and Dad says, 'Cheese'
And Dad clicks away but takes our knees
Every five minutes it's *clickety-click*
And Dad's favourite word is, can you guess what?
'Trifik, trifik, trifik!'
We go on walks to see the view
From behind a tree out jumps Dad
And says, 'I've got you!'
By now Emily is as mad as a hatter
Fed up with photos and Dad's patter
A meeting we have to decide Dad's fate
To throw in the sea or give him no tea
What a calamity that would be
Instead a vote we passed and so
We buried him deep in the sand
Where only his toe was left on show
And guess what? We took a photo!
'Trifik, trifik, trifik!'

Rebecca Gidley (11)
Lostock Hall Community High School & Arts College

Father, Dear Father

Father, dear Father, come home with me now!
The clock in the steeple strikes one,
You promised dear Father, that you would come home,
As soon as your day's work was done.
Our fire has gone out, our house is all dark
And Mother's been watching since tea,
With poor brother Benny so sick in her arms
And no one to help her, but me.

Father, dear Father, come home with me now!
The clock on the steeple strikes two,
The night has grown colder and Benny is worse,
But he has been calling for you.
Indeed he is is worse, Ma says he will die,
Perhaps before morning shall dawn
And this is the message she sent me to bring,
'Come quickly or he will be gone.'

Father, dear Father, come home with me now!
The clock in the steeple strikes three,
The house is so lonely, the hours are so long,
For poor weeping mother and me.
Yes, we are alone, poor Benny is dead
And gone with the angels of light
And these were the very last words that he said,
'I want to kiss Papa goodnight!'

Stephanie Bretherton (13)
Lostock Hall Community High School & Arts College

The Asian Earthquake

Ground shaking
Some people aren't waking
But the rest are all alert.

People dashing
The buildings crashing
On those who are led unaware.

Parents crying
Are their children dying?
Under rubble, are they in pain?

Hope, losing
They're not choosing
To be in the state they're in.

Aid is coming
The help that we bring
But how many can we save?

Over fifty-thousand lost
What a huge, immense cost
Generations never to be replaced.

Emily Birkett (11)
Lostock Hall Community High School & Arts College

The Cinema Date

There once was a girl called Kate,
Who went on a cinema date,
She thought he was cool,
So she took him to school
And he went off with her very best mate!

Kathryn Jamison (11)
Lostock Hall Community High School & Arts College

Jenny, Do You Love Me?

I love you with all my heart,
I've never told anybody this,
So I thought I should start by telling you.

I hope you don't mind
But I love you.

Every day I love you more and more
All the time I see you, my heart pounds
With my love for you.

I love you Jenny, but do you love me?
If you would be happier without me, then I will leave
Just as long as you know
I love you, yes I really do love you.

I knew this as soon as I laid my eyes upon you
For I was struck by Cupid's arrow.

While I'm writing this, I am crying,
I don't know why, I just want you to know I love you.

I have not seen you since Friday, I miss you so much
I want you to knock on my door and tell me that you love me.

I like the way you sit there in class
I like the way you walk down the path.

And when you said yes
My whole body filled with joy
As you made me the luckiest boy to ever love.

Philip Michael Whiteside (13)
Lostock Hall Community High School & Arts College

Annoying Cousins

The day ends, I come home from school
Only to be made a fool
My cousins are here, they run and scream
Annoying me, they make a terrible team.

I am tired and want to watch TV
But how much longer do they have to bug me?
A quiet minute or two is all I need
My patience has gone to seed.

I run upstairs to my room
But they come up, all too soon
I try to hide and then take a peek
They don't give time to let me speak.

In many ways I think they're great
But when I'm tired, they can wait
Before I play their little games
I want some time, or I'll go insane!

Connie Plummer (13)
St Bede's Catholic High School, Lytham

Evil Is Here!

In the depths underneath the grounds,
That's where it lurks, out of bounds,
In the shadows is where it hides,
Only revealing its deep red eyes.

Wherever you go it will follow you,
To school, to the park, believe me, it's true,
Like a stalker it creeps into the night,
Never look back, else you might get a fright.

Try not to be scared, for it feeds on your fear
And try not to worry, because evil is here!

Lucy Clements (13)
St Bede's Catholic High School, Lytham

Summer Rain

In the winding lane
After the dust and heat
Here comes the rain
In the long and colourful street.

After the dust and heat
It clatters along rooves
In the long and colourful street
Like a noisy horse's hooves.

It clatters along rooves
Splashing on the windowpane
Like a noisy horse's hooves
The rain, the summer rain.

Megan Marshall (13)
St Bede's Catholic High School, Lytham

Snow Morning

It was white that morning
Soft, silent snow lay all around
Cold and crisp delight
Stinging cheeks bright red.

Soft, silent snow lay all around
Waiting to be played in
Stinging cheeks bright red
Breath that looks like fog.

Waiting to be played in
A big, smiling snowman
Breath that looks like fog
Children's voices laughing.

A big, smiling snowman
Cold, crisp delight
Children's voices laughing
It was white that morning.

Katie Paparestis (13)
St Bede's Catholic High School, Lytham

Cup Final

It was a hot summer's day
It was the Cup Final
The month was May
Guess who's back? It's Lionel.

It was the Cup Final
The fans all coming through the turnstiles
Guess who's back? It's Lionel
The fans are all smiles.

Lionel is on the ball, he shoots and scores
The month was May
The other fans are beaten and head for the doors!
It was a hot summer's day.

Glen Martland (13)
St Bede's Catholic High School, Lytham

Springtime

Not summer, not autumn, not winter, but spring,
Colourful flowers grow in fields of green grass,
The time of year where all the birds sing
And yet how quickly the time will pass.

Colourful flowers grow in fields of green grass,
I love this season, it's come at last
And yet how quickly the time will pass,
The first of the seasons, the rest are last.

I love this season, it's come at last,
This season is beautiful, the best of them all,
The first of the seasons, the rest are last,
I will never forget it, not one bit at all.

This season is beautiful, the best of them all,
The time of year where all the birds sing,
I will never forget it, not one bit at all,
Not summer, not autumn, not winter, but spring.

Danielle Starkey (13)
St Bede's Catholic High School, Lytham

The Last Dragon

We always thought we knew it all, but in reality we have no clue
And we would stop them if we could
In a way it's pretty true
Or is it that they are misunderstood?

We would stop them if we could
From killing people in illusion
Or is it that they are misunderstood?
Really it's just confusion.

From killing people in illusion
Maybe we could make a truce
Really it's just confusion
If we mess up, hell will break loose.

I think they are cool
In a way it's pretty true
But I hope they never rule
We always thought we knew it all, but in reality we have no clue.

Nick Reilly (13)
St Bede's Catholic High School, Lytham

Come On England

Off we go to Germany next year
We're all behind you screaming loud
With all the drunks drinking beer
Do your best, we are all very proud.

Here we are, England's crowd
The victory puts us top of the group
On the plane I see the clouds
All the fans by now have turned a bit loop.

We have a better team because we're top of the group
Sven's 11 will surely be good
We're on the street, a faithful troop
Running along, like a flood.

John Travers (13)
St Bede's Catholic High School, Lytham

Christmas

Stars twinkling back and forth
Christmas light above the floor
Eating food, bring on more
Golden wrappings shoved around the floor
Waking up to a white world
Screaming and shouting through the door
Yawning and stretching, it's half-past six
The day has ended
The sun has set
Day has ended
But not yet
Kneeling and praying
Now it's ended.

Conor Rogers (11)
St Bede's Catholic High School, Lytham

Shot Down

I hate the way they shoot you down
One by one we fall
They shoot us in the middle of town
They make us feel so small.

One by one we fall
Our hearts are breaking inside us
They make us feel so small
Our family's no longer beside us.

Our hearts are breaking inside us
They're killing us off so slowly
Our family's no longer beside us
They think of us so lowly.

They're killing us off so slowly
They shoot us in the middle of town
They think of us so lowly
I hate the way they shoot us down.

Joanna Stuart (13)
St Bede's Catholic High School, Lytham

The Descent

Crisp morning, pedals start turning,
Ledges, burms, north shore and jumps,
Round all the corners, the wet mud churning,
Disc brakes squeal going over the humps.

Ledges, burms, north shore and jumps,
Little kicker into a drop,
Over the tree roots, *thump, thump, thump,*
Here comes the big drop, no point trying to stop.

Little kicker into a drop,
Handle bars are slippy with all the rain,
Here comes the big drop, no point trying to stop,
The ground is slippy because there are no drains.

Round all the corners, the wet mud churning,
Get to the bottom panting, gasping for breath,
The end of the crisp morning, wheels stop turning,
The end of a good day, but I'll be back, that's for sure.

Harrison Hazell (14)
St Bede's Catholic High School, Lytham

The Cup

We have come to win the cup
We have come to have some fun
Hopefully we won't bin our chance
We are here to stun.

We have come to have some fun
But not to mess around
We are here to stun
If we play our very best to win, we are bound.

At the moment we're on fire like burning coal
Hopefully we won't bin our chance
Shoot, *bang!* We scored a goal!
We have come to win the cup!

Michael Churchman (13)
St Bede's Catholic High School, Lytham

Shopping

It was a hot day in the middle of May,
The day that I went shopping,
Not Monday, Tuesday, Wednesday, Thursday or Friday,
But Saturday,
I picked today because I needed some new clothing.

The day that I went shopping,
I took the bus into town,
I picked today because I needed some new clothing,
I wanted something that was new and brown.

I took the bus into town,
I went into all the different shops,
I wanted something that was new and brown,
But when my money starts to run out, the fun stops!

I went into all the different shops,
Not Monday, Tuesday, Wednesday, Thursday or Friday,
But Saturday,
But when my money starts to run out, the fun stops,
It was a hot day in the middle of May.

Kim McKay (13)
St Bede's Catholic High School, Lytham

I've Got A Crush!

I've got a crush
Don't know what to say
When I see him I turn to slush
His birthday's in May.

Don't know what to say
I love him so much
His birthday's in May
He's got a soft and gentle touch.

I love him so much
I think about him all the time
He's got a soft and gentle touch
I want him to be mine.

Want to tell him how I feel
When I see him I turn to slush
I wish it was real
I've got a crush.

Natasha Holmes (13)
St Bede's Catholic High School, Lytham

Hearts And Flowers

Life isn't always full of pretty hearts and flowers,
What he told us we didn't think was true,
We sat by your hospital bed for hours,
Wishing to have lots more time with you.

What he told us we didn't think was true,
But what the doctor predicted was right,
Wishing to have lots more time with you,
Who'd have thought that would be your last night.

But what the doctor predicted was right,
We will always be thinking of you and miss you forever,
Who'd have thought that would be your last night,
We promise we will forget you never.

We will always be thinking of you and miss you forever,
We sat by your hospital bed for hours,
We promise we will forget you never,
Life isn't always full of pretty hearts and flowers.

Charlotte Vincent (15)
St Bede's Catholic High School, Lytham

Unrequited Love

When I see you I don't know what to say
I wish I could say all the things that I felt
No one understands that you blow me away
But when I see you I start to melt.

I wish I could say all the things that I felt
It hurts so much to see you there
But when I see you I start to melt
To look at you and know you don't care.

It hurts so much to see you there
I know when you looked at me I crossed your mind
To look at you and know you don't care
I just wish it could be like that every time.

I know when you looked at me I crossed your mind
No one understands that you blow me away
I just wish it could be like that every time
When I see you I don't know what to say.

Liz Winkley (15)
St Bede's Catholic High School, Lytham

Night And Day

From a cold start,
To a lighter way,
From a cloudy heart,
To a darker day.

To a lighter way,
When the sun does shine,
To a darker day,
When night draws nigh.

When the sun does shine,
Flowers do grow,
When night draws nigh,
The sun's heat will go.

Flowers do grow,
From a cloudy heart,
The sun's heat will go,
From a cold start.

Louis Shepherd (13)
St Bede's Catholic High School, Lytham

A Cloud Is . . .

Fluffy and puffy and white
It sits in a sky so bright
It looks like candyfloss
And it bounces and springs like moss.

It sits on a mountain peek
And is as soft as a baby's cheek
It is said to have a silver lining
And for happy people it can be seen shining.

It is easy to see in the light
But is hard to see at night
It looks like cotton wool
And the shapes it forms are never dull.

Andrew Hall (11)
St Bede's Catholic High School, Lytham

Nature Is Deadly

Surfing over the soft white snow
My goggles clouding up, getting hard to see
Faster and faster, away I go
Other boarders catching up to me.

My goggles clouding up, getting hard to see
Pick up speed, slide along
Other boarders catching up to me
I hear a rumble, something's wrong.

I pick up speed, slide along
Slide along, just dodged a tree
I hear a rumble, something's wrong
Snow is quickly catching up to me.

Slide along, just dodged a tree
Faster and faster, away I go
Snow is quickly catching up to me
Surfing over the soft white snow.

Peter Andrew (13)
St Bede's Catholic High School, Lytham

The Morning After!

Such a place from the night before
Sparklers, rockets and burnt out wood
Lay so still in the fog
Smells of bonfires fill the air
Hard to see in front of your face
Because of the fog and smoke all over the place!

Empty shells clutter the ground
Some still left in buckets full of sand
Everything left from the night before
From a night that was so good for all!

Elizabeth Taylor (12)
St Bede's Catholic High School, Lytham

Darkness

My heart is shrouded with nought but grim,
My eyes blaze with fear and despair.
It feels as if the night has fallen in,
I'm trapped in darkness, without a care.

My eyes blaze with fear and despair,
Why do I suffer alone at night?
I'm trapped in darkness, without a care,
My tears can no longer put up a fight.

Why do I suffer alone at night?
These nightmares show the truth and lies.
My tears can no longer put up a fight,
What is the difference, if my heart both bleeds and cries?

These nightmares show the truth and lies,
It feels as if the night has fallen in.
What is the difference, if my heart both bleeds and cries?
My heart is shrouded with nought but grim.

Zoë Morrison (15)
St Bede's Catholic High School, Lytham

Hallowe'en Is . . .

A spooky night
A bag full of sweets
A fun day out
An orange pumpkin.

Scary costumes
Ghastly faces
Sharing of your treats
Ghost's reunion.

Full moon, beware
The werewolf's near
You don't want to meet him on
Hallowe'en night!

Florence Powell (11)
St Bede's Catholic High School, Lytham

Eyes Of Tragedy

Look at the tragedy in her sad eyes
Her vacant but piercing stare
You'd think all she's capable of is hate and despise
Sadness is under that glare.

Her vacant but piercing stare
Is it to stop her heart from breaking?
Sadness is under that glare
When she cries, her world starts shaking.

Is it to stop her heart from breaking?
Is she protecting herself from harm?
When she cries, her world starts shaking
Is she protecting herself from his charm?

Is she protecting herself from harm?
You'd think all she's capable of is hate and despise
Is she protecting herself from his charm?
Look at the tragedy in her sad eyes.

Elizabeth Clements (15)
St Bede's Catholic High School, Lytham

Storm

The sky grows dark, the birds go silent,
Everything stays still, waiting, waiting,
The wind gets up, its nostrils flaring,
They start to pace across the ever-glooming sky,
It thrashes its tail, sending a violent rustle through the trees,
There's a flash of lightning, like the white of the eye
opening in the darkness,
Then they take off, racing and pounding towards us,
They come close, very close,
When they start to fade, it fades and fades,
It grows still again: its breath spent.

Karen McConachie (13)
St Bede's Catholic High School, Lytham

Heartbroken

When I see you standing there
I feel like I want to die
I just can't help but stop and stare
Then the tears flow and I start to cry.

I feel like I want to die
I've never felt like this before
Then the tears flow again and I start to cry
It's hurting to know you don't want me anymore.

I've never felt like this before
You're the one with the key to my heart
It's hurting to know you don't want me anymore
And I hate the way that we're so far apart.

You're the one with the key to my heart
I just can't help but stop and stare
And I hate the way that we're so far apart
When I see you standing there.

Kathryn Mulligan (15)
St Bede's Catholic High School, Lytham

Growing Up!

When you are five, you're on top of the world,
When you are six, you always seem to feel sick,
When you are seven, you think you're the best,
When you are eight, you seem to always be late,
When you are nine, you always shine,
When you are ten, you can buy a hen,
When you are eleven, you learn about Heaven,
When you are twelve, you start to grow up,
When you are thirteen, you have so much fun,
When you are fourteen . . . I don't know, it's only just begun!

Rebecca Laver (14)
St Bede's Catholic High School, Lytham

My Parents

My parents are so loving
(But why nag me all the time?)
They look after me, feed me and clothe me
(It's always too early in the morning!)
I look so much like them
(School on Monday?)
Most of the time they are right
(In my view they are always wrong!)
Taking me everywhere
(We've been to a museum already this year!)

My parents are so loving
(They are also so embarrassing!)
Holidays, anywhere in the world
(Why can't we go anywhere hot though?)
Christmas, lots of presents
(Another jumper, I've already got 10 off you!)
Always there when you need them
(I can walk to school on my own, I'm not stupid!)
Thanks Mum and Dad for being so good
(Most of the time anyway!)

Alex Aitken (13)
St Bede's Catholic High School, Lytham

Snow - Haiku

Beautiful petals,
Dancing in the bare sunlight,
Floating swiftly down.

Mercedes De Pascual Cardiel (14)
St Bede's Catholic High School, Lytham

World Cup Qualifiers

World Cup here we come
It's good to win the cup
Everyone's here to have some fun
It would bring our spirits up.

It's good to win the cup
I love that trophy so much
It would bring our spirits up
More so if I could have a touch.

I love that trophy so much
It would be good to have it all the time
We always beat the Dutch
I just want it to be mine.

So Germany, here we come
We're here to nick the fun
We'll have more than some
Especially in the sun.

David Jakes
St Bede's Catholic High School, Lytham

Sky

Blue like a baby's eyes,
Like a huge, big bed sheet,
There is no sound, there is silence,
Mixed smells hovering in the air,
Looks soft and welcoming and homely,
It has no taste, only the candyfloss that floats around all day,
Planes leaving marks like a ruler on a page
And the sun that is smiling all day,
Then goes down at night.

Charlotte Newsham (11)
St Bede's Catholic High School, Lytham

My Sister

I didn't ask for her to come along,
No, no, why would I want a sister?
I was happy on my own,
Why did I have to have a sister?

But then she was born . . .
Oh, I fell in love!
She was adorable
And was my sister!

'Scream, scream, scream!'
Would you just shut up!
I'm trying to sleep,
Why did I have to have a sister?

Now eight years old,
Big and bold,
She can be annoying,
But deep down, I love her so!

Adriana Garrad (13)
St Bede's Catholic High School, Lytham

Sky

The sky is blue
Like a bit of sea
With the clouds making shapes
One is a mad cow.

Some of the cloud pictures are dogs
I have a dog
It hogs the floor
It is the best dog ever.

The clouds look like candyfloss
I like candyfloss
It is a handy cost
Everyone should like candyfloss.

John Winthrop (11)
St Bede's Catholic High School, Lytham

The Wind

When I hear his gentle voice
I always think he's a ghost.
And he always says to me:
'Hello, I'm your friend, the wind.'

He always blows towards me
when he wants to talk with me.
And I always answer him
if he wants to play with me.

I've never seen my friend the wind,
but I always know where he is.
The wind never dies
'cause he's God's right hand.

When the wind goes to sleep
I say goodnight to him with a kiss
Oh, my friend, the wind,
I wish you good dreams.

Paloma Poveda (11)
St Bede's Catholic High School, Lytham

Hallowe'en

Vampires and ghosts sweep the streets
While greedy children go looking for sweets
The 31st is the date
So be careful because of fate.

Fun and games for everyone
But they all stop when the clock strikes one
Thunder and lightning is upon us
Surely now, we're goners!

Now comes the finale of the night
This should give you a terrible fright
So make sure you're always weary
Because on Hallowe'en things get *scary!*

Lauren Jackson (11)
St Bede's Catholic High School, Lytham

Winter

Winter is as white as snow
The darker nights, the stars that glow
Christmas is coming soon
The blinding light of the shining moon.

No more playing outside after school
The wind is cold, draughty and cruel
In the morning the sky is its darkest blues
The falling snow crunches on the bottom of our shoes.

The robins that go *tweet, tweet, tweet*
Go hopping along the cold white street
But soon it will be spring again
So goodbye snow and hello rain.

Daniella Tierney (11)
St Bede's Catholic High School, Lytham

Clouds Are . . .

It's a fluffy pillow,
Made of candyfloss,
Hurts your teeth,
See the dentist after.

Men help fluff the pillow,
Women sleep on them,
Feels like hair that's just been washed,
Washed by a hairdresser.

Dried by a hairdryer,
Hair that was wet,
Then was damp
And cold as well.

Very hot,
Like the sun
And the moon
Are friends with the stars.

Harriet Bower (11)
St Bede's Catholic High School, Lytham

The Sun

A great ball of fire,
A blinding sight,
It hangs like a spider,
It is so bright.

A big illumination,
A meteor above,
It is such an inspiration,
A view that I love.

It pops and crackles,
It shines like a star,
It really, really dazzles,
A light from afar.

It rises in the morning,
Like a golden sphere,
It sets in the evening,
It is rather queer.

Zoe Moreton (11)
St Bede's Catholic High School, Lytham

Blackpool

The place where I live
Is great and the best
It has everything to give
And it's here in the west.
There's a Golden Mile
And a wonderful prom
You're greeted with a smile
No matter where you come from.
It's simply the best
I'll say it's just cool
And now you have guessed
It's breezy Blackpool!

Sophie Mina (11)
St Bede's Catholic High School, Lytham

Panther

Black as the witching hour
Mysterious and cunning
Feared by many
A predator of the jungle.

Sleek as silk
So lithe and lean
Its coat gleams silver
Reflected from the moon.

Eyes like headlamps
Seeking out prey
You can't outsmart her
There is no escape.

Walks like a model
Full of dignity and pride
A superior creature
Threatening and sly.

Cait Kielty-Adey (13)
St Bede's Catholic High School, Lytham

Snow

What is white and cold?
What makes you shiver
And chills your body?
It comes in winter
Sometimes at Christmas
It falls as snowflakes
Out of the sky
And covers the ground
In a white blanket
Snowmen, snow fights
All children's delights
My favourite time of year.

Katie Mitchell (12)
St Bede's Catholic High School, Lytham

Parents

You can't live with them,
But you can't live without them.
Parents are always there for you when you are sad,
But sometimes they drive us mad.
Parents like to groan
And they always seem to moan.

They're always very serious,
I'd rather they kissed and cuddled
And joked about and laughed.
As least we can say that everything's OK,
When Mum and Dad are daft.

Holidays are sometimes fun,
As long as we are not visiting war graves . . .
Again.
Thank you Mum and Dad for being there,
Most of the time, anyway!

Myles Swindlehurst (13)
St Bede's Catholic High School, Lytham

Music

Music is so wild
It makes me want to shout out loud!
To dance on the rooftops
To scream to the sky
Music is what makes my dance moves fly!
I step to the left
I step to the right
I jump to the front
I jump in the light!
So don't forget . . .
Music is *what makes my life!*

Aimee-Lee Dean (11)
St Bede's Catholic High School, Lytham

On The Stage

I have always wanted to be on the stage
Learning my lines, page by page
Rehearsals all the time
Practising every line
Doing my best to impress.

As the audience poured in
I couldn't wait to begin
I just knew it was nigh
As my parents were in sight.

As the act came to an end
I could hear the loud cheers from my friends.

I went home that night
Filled with delight
I went to sleep feeling proud
That I had impressed the handsome crowd.

I soon drifted away
Until the next day
When I had to once again
Perform in the play!

Jenny Doyle (13)
St Bede's Catholic High School, Lytham

A Boogie Woogie Spider

Spiders love to go dancing
And boogie around all day
They scream and shout
If anyone gets in their way
They love to wear ballet shoes
And dance to music all day
They hate it when they have to stop
And tidy all their things away.

Ellie Dugdale (11)
St Bede's Catholic High School, Lytham

The Things That Lurk In My Room

The things that lurk in my room
Oh, now where did I put that broom?
There're socks everywhere and what is that?
I think it's my toothbrush, *eewww,* it's a dead rat!

Now I really can't be bothered, it takes so long
What is that smell? Now that is wrong!
I swore I saw something run across the floor!
Quick, catch it, *aww!* now it's out the door!

I think this pizza is three weeks old
Oh well, I'll just scrape off the mould!
I think I found my hamster, what a relief,
Oh my God! It's last week's beef!

Now I must be honest, I do confess
I like my room being a complete mess!

Jerome Sanderson (13)
St Bede's Catholic High School, Lytham

When I'm Old

One rainy day I was told
What I'll be like when I'm old.

My head will go pruney and my brains will turn to mush
I'll become more wrinkly than George W Bush.

Grey hairs will sprout out of my nose
And I'll grow mould between my toes.

I'll sit around with my fellow fogies
Pickin' my nose and flickin' my bogies.

I remember when my granny said
'You'll wake up one mornin' and you'll be as good as dead!'

Daniel Wilson (12)
St Bede's Catholic High School, Lytham

Pop Idol

Me and my mates, we went in and saw,
The judges sat there, I ran for the door.

My friends pulled me back, there was nowhere to hide,
I had to release my voice from inside.

My face showed fear, I tried not to show,
This was it now, did we stay in or go?

'Yes from me,' 'Yes,' and 'Yes.'
We got through the round with complete success.

The next round was hard, we all found it tough,
We had practised loads, we were all looking rough!

We got through to the final, we kept going strong,
We were thinking that showbiz was where we belonged.

Our final performance, our final song,
Was showbiz really, where our group belonged.

The judges said yes, we were in with a chance,
We were all so excited, we wanted to dance!

The votes flooded in, we were pacing the floor,
Would we win and be famous, or shown through the door?

The moment of truth . . . success it was ours!
We were showered with kisses and bombarded with flowers!

We sung once again with smiles and with cheer,
The nerves had all gone, applause was all we could hear!

Megan Davis (13)
St Bede's Catholic High School, Lytham

There's Something There!

Laughing, joking, with all my mates,
Time's ticking on and it's getting late,
I say goodbye and head for the door,
I should have been home two hours ago.

Out on the street, I start to walk,
I cut through the forest,
It's quicker that way,
A rustling sound makes me jump.

There was something there, watching me,
I could feel its eyes following me everywhere I went,
I carried on walking, getting faster and faster,
Its feet were thudding heavily, like a tree trunk falling to the floor.

Out on the street again, I start to run,
It's catching up, getting quicker and quicker,
I stumble and fall, I need to get up,
It's only a few metres away.

Back on my feet, running again,
I'm getting tired, slowing down,
I need to rest, but I can't,
It leaps towards me and knocks me down.

It's pinning me down, can't move at all,
Sharp teeth coming towards me,
It rips at my throat,
All I saw before I died were the deep yellow eyes of the wolf.

Vicki Harrap (13)
St Bede's Catholic High School, Lytham

The Joys Of Home

I sit alone
And think of home,
Silence drumming in my ears,
Done nothing wrong,
I just sit and long
For home.

The good old days
When the sun's bright rays
Shone down
Around
The big fig tree
In the garden
And
Drink in hand
I would talk and play
Every day
With my friends.

And then,
At night
The light grows dim,
Revealing stars,
Saturn and Mars,
The moon;
And very soon
I'll be back,
Home,
Free to roam
The joys of life.

Rory McCann (14)
St Bede's Catholic High School, Lytham

25th Set Skating Incident

I took a run up
To the massive set,
Twenty-five in total
It was the biggest yet.

I pushed and got right to the edge
And had placed my feet,
I bent my knees and kickflipped
But my kickflip wasn't clean.

I was flying through the air
At the speed of light,
I crashed on my board,
From a terrible height.

I was unconscious for awhile
Until I came awake,
I saw my snapped board
And chucked it in the lake.

I went into the city
And bought a new board,
Then I started to skate
Even though people roared.

I attempted the set again
This was my final try,
I kickflipped to the bottom
And landed on a guy.

Matt Jackson (13)
St Bede's Catholic High School, Lytham

Fear For Freedom

I promised not to tell a soul
They were there in the shed,
Waiting for the right time,
Every day, in total fear and alarm;
A secret between me and Benjamin.

He was to lead them, all twelve,
Out over the French mountains into Spain,
I helped, trying my best,
The moonlit sky lighting the path,
A path to freedom and life.

His hair was thin and dirty,
A beard thick like woven sheep's wool,
His smile ear to ear,
A kind loving heart which was needed at this time -
A time of patience and tension.

I fed them and kept them company,
In the cold, dark cave,
Going against my family's will;
A true Catholic, helping Jews.
I watched them safely stepping into a new country . . .

. . . where fear was far, like Benjamin,
Left behind.
A cold rush of adrenalin passed through me,
Like a bullet through a body,
Not everyone successful, Benjamin gone . . .
His life, instead of the children's.

Rebecca Holdsworth (13)
St Bede's Catholic High School, Lytham

Volcano

The volcano, a lava world,
The volcano is very hot,
An old
Mountain, a form of boiling pot.

The volcano, an explosion,
A firework and an
Erosion.

A water river,
A forest life.
A lava river,
A forest die.

The volcano,
Infernal dream.
The volcano,
A great scream.

The volcano,
A scary thing,
It terrifies everything.

If you watch it,
Far away, you could see
A fire way.

The dynamited,
Have been burnt down
And of this form.
I have finished it,
On my own.

Emilio Poveda (11)
St Bede's Catholic High School, Lytham

Free Run

Down the highway
Over the fence
Into a hole
Made by a mole.

They're gaining on me
As I enter WHSmith
Onto the top floor
My legs are sore.

Out the window
I climb the drain
Onto the roof
My plan is foil proof.

I grab the wire
And slide down
Through double glazing
I feel amazing.

Bang!
I get shot
I cannot move
I can hear the phone booth.

Tick-tock
The bomb explodes
There's nothing I can do
The noise is like a zoo.

Now my run is over
I'm lying here dead
But I'll be back
You have my word on that!

Sam Bilsborough (14)
St Bede's Catholic High School, Lytham

Selflessness

The rush of blood down my arm
Falling *drip* . . . in my palm.

The crimson flow stains my skin
I push deeper with my pin.

Cutting harder, deeper still
It's addictive, like a pill.

A crazy high in my head
Soon enough I will be dead.

My bloody friend this little knife
Slowly, slowly, takes my life.

A pool of blood on the floor
Cutting, slicing, more and more.

My life does flash
But I still slash
Hoping for the end.

'Cause all that's left in this world,
Is me and my little friend.

Charlie Moore (13)
St Bede's Catholic High School, Lytham

What?

A withered hand, closed tightly around a splinter of wood
A flickering, yellow flame, licking the fingers of darkness
An emerald eye, staring into the light
A shroud of darkness, wrapped around a body of shadows
A draught
Nothing.

Emily Eccles (13)
St Bede's Catholic High School, Lytham

War

I waited in the trench with a gun in my hand,
It was the M1092 brand,
Gunfire and explosions were all around,
The noise was a terrible sound.

'Come on boys!' It was time to go,
It was the time of sheer sorrow.
I took what may be my last two breaths,
As I followed the others to our deaths.

I jumped and climbed out of the trench,
All I could smell was a dead body stench.
I saw my followers fall in pain,
We were no longer sane.

Only me and seven others were left on no-man's-land,
It was not exactly what we had planned.
Suddenly, as a meteor-like object hit the ground,
There was no more sound . . .

Mikey Jones (14)
St Bede's Catholic High School, Lytham

Edward Dragon

E dward sleeps through the year
D reaming peacefully, without fear
W histling through his scaly nose
A sudden twitch from his toes
R oaring and grunting, as he snores
D anger as he stretches his claws

D eadly roaring day and night
R eady to put up a fierce fight
A ngrily he spits out flames
G roaning on about his pains
O n his own he feels so sorry
N obody knows he watches Corrie!

Jasmine Sanderson (12)
St Bede's Catholic High School, Lytham

The Bird

I see the bird in its tree
I hear the bird singing to me
I see the bird soar through the sky
The bird sees me as it passes by.

I like to hear the bird's sweet song
In the morn as I walk along
Down the path and up the hill
The bird follows me, it always will.

Harriet Aspinall (12)
St Bede's Catholic High School, Lytham

A River's Journey

I am running quickly down the hill
Heading for the estuary.
I swerve from side to side
Getting faster and faster.
I go over rocks, through the grasses
The rocks, they follow me.
As I head faster towards the open space
Waiting for my journey's end,
The roughest ride of my life.
Down, down, down, I go,
Getting faster and faster,
Closer and closer.
The estuary now not far to go
I think of the wonderful things I will see.
The stillness until the open sea
Then still at last as my journey stops.
So still, so peaceful, so me.

Elizabeth Kenny (12)
St Bede's Catholic High School, Lytham

Smile

When you're feeling down and wearing a frown,
Just give a little smile and it will all be worthwhile.
Someone out there, even if you don't know where,
Needs your smile, to make their day worthwhile.
It's been tough and you feel you've had enough,
You want to go home, but you're all alone.

Then you see a shining smile break through
And this smile which is meant just for you.
So you smile and the craze has started,
Even though you and Mr Wrong have just parted.

The sun breaks through and is beaming on you,
So now you feel that there's nothing you can't do.
Your day becomes brighter and your worries lighter,
You have suddenly become a very strong fighter.
You turn your frown upside down,
Making you feel like you're wearing a crown.

And so now don't forget these words of wisdom,
A smile you can give is very cheap,
But the smile you get back is there to keep.

Aimee Carr (15)
St Bede's Catholic High School, Lytham

Forest

The gentle sensation of the silent forest
The wandering beast scuttles through its territory
The soft flow of the clear river
The branches that waft in the dead of night
The silent mist that covers everything.

Katie Thomson (12)
St Bede's Catholic High School, Lytham

Fire!

I started it all when I sent a single cinder
Into the corner of the baker's shop
I eventually crept upstairs like a silent leopard hunting its prey
I then claimed my first victim while he was quietly sleeping
And then I burnt him until his skin peeled off
I then set the bakery alight
And watched it smoulder into the ground
With my demon-red eyes
I started to watch people staring in despair
But I don't really care
I then started to reach out with my blazing arms
To grasp all the houses at the side of me
I then started to spread across London like lightning
Setting everything in my path on fire
I looked behind me and all of London was ablaze
But then people started to throw water on me
I am now feeling very woozy
Because I am losing energy
I am dying
I am dead!

Sam Robert Currie (11)
St Edmund Arrowsmith Catholic High School, Ashton-in-Makerfield

Sunlight

I am driving the car and the sun is blazing in my eyes
I was being blinded by the shining sun
I was looking at the sun. It was orange and yellow
I was sat in the sun. It tans people's bodies
I was on the beach. The sand was hot
Because of the big orange and yellow sun
I look up in the sky, it was sparkling
I saw it glowing from the shadow
I am blinded by the sun raining on us
I am a circle in the sky
I find the sun coming bright at me.

Katie Richardson (11)
St Edmund Arrowsmith Catholic High School, Ashton-in-Makerfield

Fire

Fire blazing sinisterly
Highly frightened people
I have killed a little boy
I don't care what I destroy
People watch in despair
I don't mind, I do what I want
I burn houses
I kill things
I'm what everyone's scared of
I cause pain and I love it
I cause heartbreaks, I don't care
I see people running
I shall chase
I eventually find them
They burn like coal
All that's left is an ash
Every kill I do, I get more energy
I am stronger than ever.

Matthew Houghton (11)
St Edmund Arrowsmith Catholic High School, Ashton-in-Makerfield

Sunlight

I rise in the morning, which the people love
I am a big fireball in the sky above
I am so hot some people get a tan
I also make others need a fan
I am so hot that the heat is everywhere
I do not bother some people, they don't care
I am so tired it is nearly time for me to go down
I can then make the kids frown
I am setting now, goodbye
I think today I made some people fry!

Jessica Gates (11)
St Edmund Arrowsmith Catholic High School, Ashton-in-Makerfield

Frost

I swooped along the lake leaving a trail of ice on the lake
I made icicles twinkle in the cave
I made the road slippery on those cold winter days
I made your feet cold while you were in bed
I made you shiver and shake
I brought back those happy days of snowball fights
And those cuddles on a cold winter's night
I made the spiders' webs glisten in the sunlight
I gave you those moments that you skated on the ice
That you wanted it to last forever
I gave you snow days when it was school
I formed the snowflakes that are all different kinds of shapes
I gave the water its gleaming coat
I made the water freeze that was at the side of your bed.

Dale Monks (11)
St Edmund Arrowsmith Catholic High School, Ashton-in-Makerfield

Fire

I saw the cooker on
I thought the humans would be gone
I picked up some paper
The person that called them was the neighbour
I see the humans crying
But soon they will be dying
In the kitchen it's *red*
I go upstairs to make them *dead*
I go in the parent's room
To send them to their doom
They try to run
For me it's bunches of fun
I make them fry
But I see water and it's my turn to die!

Daniel Wood (11)
St Edmund Arrowsmith Catholic High School, Ashton-in-Makerfield

Mary, By Liz

I know a whacky girl who likes Mcfly
And doesn't like Arsenal or Thierry,
Although we don't always see eye to eye,
She's the one and only, my friend Mary.

She was born in June, is 14 years old,
Everything she says and does make me laugh,
She will be an actress, so I am told,
Mary is a bit of a psychopath!

Although she is loud and sings every day,
I suppose that I could put up with it,
She's a jolly good fellow, as they say,
Because of her kind heart, big smile and wit!

So that's enough on Mary, you'll agree,
You'll have to ask her what she thinks of me!

Liz Dooner (14)
St Edmund Arrowsmith Catholic High School, Ashton-in-Makerfield

Sunlight

I wake up early in the morning
Making everywhere light
I give people suntans
Melt their ice creams
I also grow plants
Make everyone happy
I am the sparkle in the sea
I am yellow, orange, red
I have done my day of work
It is time for me to go now
Bye-bye!

Zoe Brown (11)
St Edmund Arrowsmith Catholic High School, Ashton-in-Makerfield

Sweet Shop

I enter the sweet shop on the main street,
All the children are eating chocolate,
I need to buy a treat for me to eat,
If I eat it all I will be quite fat.

I am under quite a lot of pressure,
I'm taking too much time to mix and match,
Then I see a massive pink Refresher,
At two pound for one there must be a catch.

I see a never-ending gobstopper,
It's going to make my jaw really ache,
Through the door enters a nasty shopper,
All my sweets and chocolate he does take.

I only have left a bag of Quavers,
For my friend who always does me favours.

Adam Brennan (14)
St Edmund Arrowsmith Catholic High School, Ashton-in-Makerfield

Fire

I was born yesterday from a cigarette
I crawled along the arm of the visitor's chair very slowly
I fell silently on the floor
I edged my way to the kitchen
Where I then charcoaled the tea
I filled the room in thick black smoke
And made the little girl cough loudly
I whimpered into the bathroom and melted all the taps
I then cornered the teddy bear
Well no, just the ashes
I slowly fade away through an invisible wall.

Amelia Rose Hurst (11)
St Edmund Arrowsmith Catholic High School, Ashton-in-Makerfield

A Sunlight Fright

I light up the sky with my glimmering body
I gracefully prance through the sky
Turning white people pink by the second
I carefully prey through the white blanket of clouds
Picking my next victims to tan with my hot, flaming breath
I will not give in to the rain blowing against my glamorous face
I am dancing in the rain, leaving a beautiful rainbow
Carving a bridge over the river
I light up the flowers and leave for the moon
To take the dark night through
I finally set and sleep behind
The shimmering hill of plants and rivers.

Jessica Craven (11)
St Edmund Arrowsmith Catholic High School, Ashton-in-Makerfield

Fire!

I am a weak energy source
I catch hold of an electric wire
I grow bigger
I reach for the doors, burning through to reach the other side
To burn and smoulder
I run to the television, I can't resist
I feed on the electrical source
I feed more and more and I am getting bigger by the minute
I hear the sirens of the fire engine
I feel weaker, I am getting smaller and smaller
My flames become smoke
I get smaller by the second
I am gone.

Chantelle Lowe (11)
St Edmund Arrowsmith Catholic High School, Ashton-in-Makerfield

Wind

When there's wind in the trees
The leaves dance in the breeze.

When there's wind in the water
The waves crash and slaughter.

When there's wind in the mountains
The streams flow into fountains.

When there's wind in the night
It can give such a fright.

When God thought about wind, it was a definite, 'I should'
And it can be either bad or good.

Wind is a thing that we all know about
It is normally a breeze and shouldn't make us shout.

The power of wind could uproot a tree
And without even trying could even pick up me.

Just to think about wind and what it can do
One day it could be affecting you'

Daniel Nickson (12)
St Edmund Arrowsmith Catholic High School, Ashton-in-Makerfield

Fire

I started off as just a little baby
Time flew by, in a matter of seconds, I was grown up
I was eventually bigger than my house and had to move out
I walked down the street to the shop
I decided to have a cigarette and the smoke flew over my head
I got into the shop and the shopkeeper collapsed
I seemed to get older and bigger by the minute
I looked around, for some reason the village fell down
I saw red trucks coming to me in the distance
I felt rain, then I turned around and the trucks were firing at me
I felt like I was getting younger, until I was no more.

Alex O'Neill (11)
St Edmund Arrowsmith Catholic High School, Ashton-in-Makerfield

My Last Lesson In Maths

I sit in maths, nearly falling asleep
We start statistics; it's hard to understand
I'm sat next to Russell, nicknamed The Sheep
I answer a question and raise my hand.

The lesson drags on, I begin to switch off
I glare out the window, sun shining in
I remember my sweets and start to scoff
Got a good aim, wrappers straight in the bin.

Start to brighten up, the day is ending
Got to pack away and do this first
Got to text my mum, the message is sending
I start to run out, I am never last.

The bell is ringing; it's all a mad rush
Taking the short-cut, running through the bush.

Anthony Griffiths (14)
St Edmund Arrowsmith Catholic High School, Ashton-in-Makerfield

Frost

I walk quietly in the night and leave behind a silver trail
For the day to come
I tiptoe in the early morning, touch the green grass
And then turn it into dew
I blow the fragile spiderwebs, suddenly they sparkle
I glue the door to its frozen hinges
I make the humans shiver and freeze
I turn to flakes in the cold winter weather
I climb the fading summer flowers
They instantly wilt and die
I am a friend of deadly pneumonia
I hate the dreaded sunlight
I suddenly fade away and disappear.

Ashlea Hargreaves (12)
St Edmund Arrowsmith Catholic High School, Ashton-in-Makerfield

The Deep Blue

My head spun,
My feet swelled in the minus temperatures of the water,
Each ripple of water found its way down my throat,
I was starting to feel weak underneath the midday sun
And now it started to become clear
The pain and suffering would soon come to the end,
A hissing alerted me, but not enough to wake me
From the deep sleep of hallucination,
The tattered and incredibly bright orange life jacket
That, until now, had kept me afloat, was the problem,
The hissing was a small pierce on the left hand side
Of the three and a half day old life jacket,
It was time,
Time to go down, underneath the endless moving waves
And I will sink, down into the bottomless waters
The unknown
Not even trying to stop the oncoming disaster
I waited,
I waited calmly,
Slowly picturing in my mind
The past 26 years of my life and the people
Who took place in it.

Emma Ryder (11)
St Edmund Arrowsmith Catholic High School, Ashton-in-Makerfield

Best Young Poet Trophy

I waited all night to be given out,
Into the hands of my possessor,
I launch out of my winner's hands in excitement,
I luckily landed and didn't smash,
I felt a warm hand on my handle,
I was warm all the way home,
I was put on display for everyone to see,
I went back to be won again.

Simon Williams (11)
St Edmund Arrowsmith Catholic High School, Ashton-in-Makerfield

Dark Love

Your rose, so crimson, poisoned with deep black
Just like our love, in that poison will drown
Your eyes, swallowing my will to hold back
So I let myself fall forever down.

Fall within the sharp grip of the cold night
Why aren't I happy with the love I chose?
Love is supposed to shine the greatest light
You poisoned me and our love with that rose.

If I live, should I be living for love?
But your lips were the first ones to touch mine
And made me soar high in the clouds above
But evil in your heart ripped open mine.

But I will sleep in silence, with you lie
Love you with my soul, watch the darkness die.

Beth Cunningham (14)
St Edmund Arrowsmith Catholic High School, Ashton-in-Makerfield

The Frost

I come in like a prowling wolf
I know what I make a move for
I can freeze anything
I approach swift as lightning without warning
I swoop in like a prowling hawk
I form icicles like daggers
I blow heat away with my icy breath
Nothing can stop me
Until . . .
The sun comes out
Aarrgghh! How it burns!

Patrick Ollerton (11)
St Edmund Arrowsmith Catholic High School, Ashton-in-Makerfield

Junk

I love junk, junk loves me,
So stop going on about being healthy!
Chocolate Buttons, Milky Stars
After that, it's four Mars bars.

One tooth lost and a trip to the dentist
I love junk, junk loves me
So stop going on about being healthy!

Chips and crisps they taste the same
My friend gave them to me, so I'm not to blame.

My jeans are tight, they barely fit,
Eat some more and forget it,
I love junk, junk loves me
So stop going on about being healthy!

Burgers and hot dogs, *yum, yum, yum*
Can't get enough inside my tum!

I've lost a tooth, I look a state
It's all because of what I ate
I love junk, junk loves me
I wish I'd thought about being healthy!

Charlotte Cunliffe (11)
St Edmund Arrowsmith Catholic High School, Ashton-in-Makerfield

Fire

I am a huge flame
I am red all over
I'll burn you till you're ashes
I glow like a lamp
I have lots of sparks
I get people's attention
I burn you all the time
I spread all over you
I am hot
I will kill you!

Kirsty Leanne Briscoe (11)
St Edmund Arrowsmith Catholic High School, Ashton-in-Makerfield

My School

Walk in school, loud noises everywhere,
Buildings all around, teachers marking books,
Boys playing football, while girls watch and stare,
Childish teenagers giving dirty looks.

The bell rings for lesson, everyone sighs,
Not done my homework, it's too hard for me,
Should I say I've forgot it or make up lies?
Honesty is best; it works well for me.

Got my favourite lessons, double art at last,
But the best lesson always goes quickly,
Got dreaded French next, I hope that goes fast,
Wishing the teacher's absent, that would do the trick.

But the bell's gone, the end of the day,
I'll be so happy, no longer have to stay.

Rebecca Lyon (14)
St Edmund Arrowsmith Catholic High School, Ashton-in-Makerfield

The Black Stallion

His long, black mane flashes by
Just caught a glimpse from the corner of my eye.
I know he's out there running free
I wonder if he notices me.

He makes his home in the wild
From forest glen to mountain high
Oh, how I wish that he was mine!

To take his freedom and drag him away
From all that he has seen today.
When he's running and jumping so high
The jet-black stallion will remain free
I wonder if he notices me.

Lindsay Joy Warburton (11)
St Edmund Arrowsmith Catholic High School, Ashton-in-Makerfield

Fire

I am lying helplessly on the ground
Crowded by people who soon turn to bed
I'm left alone in a dry woodland
The air is thick with heat
I can't help myself to run free
But I have no power to use and I am dying
A branch falls on me which is lying on a leaf bush
My temptation takes over and I leap to the branch
I spread along it and eat my way to the bush
I am so hungry, so I take the entire bush
Flicking my tongue at trees, branches and leaves
I grow and grow but I don't stop
I want more and soon I reach the tiny cabins of campers
Slowly I destroy and peel the bark
And clothes and flesh of some campers
I am angry how they prison me
And chase the survivors who flee to the lake
I'm soon an unstoppable energy spreading like a wild being
Supported by the wind, like a long known friend
I soon approach the lake and can't stop
I'm going to die
But I'm too late, I hit the surface
And lose my life at an amazing rate
And soon I am nothing.

Megan Concah (11)
St Edmund Arrowsmith Catholic High School, Ashton-in-Makerfield

Our Big Day

Our first day at high school,
It's a big day for us,
The alarm clock goes off,
We run for the bus.

The school is so big,
We'll all need a map,
We got up so early,
We could do with a nap.

We all look so smart,
In our new ties and coats,
We're all so nervous,
We have lumps in our throats.

The bell starts to ring,
We go to our room.
We meet our new teacher,
Our work will start soon.

We begin to write,
In our shiny new books.
If we start to talk,
He'll give one of his looks!

Our first day is over,
Our adventure has begun.
High school's not so bad,
It can really be fun!

Andrew Leigh (11)
St Edmund Arrowsmith Catholic High School, Ashton-in-Makerfield

Netball

The changing room is empty
The players start to arrive
The feeling of excitement begins to grow inside.
Adrenaline is pumping
Time to start the match
Just enough time to practise one last catch.
The whistle has been blown
The first pass has taken place
The crowd are already cheering
And the players are throwing at a fast pace.
We're in the shooting area
Always got an eye on the ball
Looking at the post, what's that?
Oh, it's a *goal*!
Three for us
Two for them
The whistle blows again.
Just in time to call half-time
Before we play again.
The second half is full of sparks
The championship nearly ended.
The post in front, she quickly tries to bend it
The shot is blocked
The crowd are shocked
The whistle blows to end it
The score's the same
We win again!

Stephanie Shaw (11)
St Edmund Arrowsmith Catholic High School, Ashton-in-Makerfield

I Wish

I wish I could see you,
I wish you were mine,
I hope for a name,
Every Valentine.

I get up early
And then I receive
A present from you
On what to believe?
Are you my mum?
Are you my dad?
Should I feel good? Should I feel bad?
My heart is breaking, Oh, I'm so sad.

For every year on the same day
You refuse a name
Oh, please ease my pain.

A number to call
Or something like that
I know you love me
I just want a chat.

So if you really, really do care
Your feelings for me
Will continue to share.

Emma Lee (11)
St Edmund Arrowsmith Catholic High School, Ashton-in-Makerfield

Swimming!

Swimming is my favourite thing,
It keeps me fit and healthy,
When I go to the Olympics,
I am sure I will get wealthy,
It will make my parents very proud,
To see me with a medal,
I will keep dreaming,
Until one day it will come true,
Until then, I will try and try again,
To make this dream come true.

Emma Greenhalgh (11)
St Edmund Arrowsmith Catholic High School, Ashton-in-Makerfield

Friends

Friends are the best
They're better than the rest
To me they're more valuable than a treasure chest.

Some friends are cool
Unlike school
School is *really* uncool.

So that's what I say
Every day, every day
In every possible way.

Friends are cool
Unlike school
So please don't be a fool
And think that friends are uncool.

Nathanial Kerfoot (11)
St Edmund Arrowsmith Catholic High School, Ashton-in-Makerfield

Someone Or Something

Dazzling, shining, shimmering,
In the light of the sun,
The spiders' webs shine.

Dazzling, shining, shimmering
In the light of the moon,
The spiders' webs gleam.

The animals make their way,
Across the garden quietly so no one can hear,
But something, somewhere is watching.

Claire Ashton (11)
St Edmund Arrowsmith Catholic High School, Ashton-in-Makerfield

Spin Bowling

For me, cricket has much heart,
Spin bowling being its greatest art.
Many great batsmen have been out,
With the spin bowling and moving about.

Some bowlers will bowl the ball wider,
But spin bowlers will bowl the odd slider.
When they bowl the ball in the rough,
It makes the batsman's job more tough.

The name Shane Warne make people scream,
When he tears apart their favourite team.
Without a doubt he is the best,
When he took 600 wickets more than the rest.

Some say cricket is a boring game,
But to me that is a real shame.
I love it when a batsman is caught,
Because cricket is England's national sport.

Thomas Pantak (11)
St Edmund Arrowsmith Catholic High School, Ashton-in-Makerfield

Horses

Clip-clop, clip-clop,
Go the horse's hooves.
Watch it gallop over the field
Neighing as it moves.

Swish-flick, swish-flick,
Whips the horse's tail.
Oh, the flies annoy it so,
Trying to bite, but fail.

Bang, bang, bang, bang,
Go the horse's feet.
As they kick the stable door
To reach their sugarbeet.

Quiet, silence, quiet, silence,
On the busy farm.
This is the peaceful time of day,
When everything is calm.

Kate Halliday (11)
St Edmund Arrowsmith Catholic High School, Ashton-in-Makerfield

Netball

You can't just pretend
You have to be cunning
To be able to defend
You have to like running
You're running on court
As a not so good pass
Unfortunately falls short
And you fall straight on your ass
You leap into the air to catch
The very slippery ball
As the umpire calls
For the end of the match
She blows the whistle
Like a very loud thistle.

Milaina Sian Bretherton (12)
St Edmund Arrowsmith Catholic High School, Ashton-in-Makerfield

Gymnastics

Gymnastics is cool, all the bars and beams,
Learning cartwheels, handstands and double flips,
Being a gymnast is one of my dreams,
Fun competitions and going on trips.

Spring boards, vaults, but the trampolines are the best,
The tumblers are great I wish I could do that,
We've got to work hard get ready for our test,
But I remember that bad fall, thank goodness for that mat.

Doing fab routines and dances as well,
Showing the judges is quite nerve-racking,
How embarrassing it would be if you fell,
But just be brave and get over with that thing.

Gymnastics is cool, all the bars and beams,
But being a gymnast is just one of my dreams.

Alex Devany (12)
St Edmund Arrowsmith Catholic High School, Ashton-in-Makerfield

St Helen's Rugby Team

Here they come, champion super Saints
The best team ever to play rugby
When they see them, the opposition faints
Because they're the best and that's how it should be.

Now the super Saints are on the pitch
It is Saints' turn now to do a great kick
Already tackled, one has got a stitch
Thinking they're good, heading for the sticks.

We've got the ball and get a cool try!
Waving around the beautiful ball
You hear all the great crowd cry
The referee makes a great try call.

The losing opposition looks so foul
'We're the best ever,' the mighty Saints growl!

Josh Stanley (12)
St Edmund Arrowsmith Catholic High School, Ashton-in-Makerfield

Holidays

School is over and I get on the plane
I know that my holiday is not far
I look out the window and I see Spain
I picture that drink waiting at the bar.

I am sat on the fresh, warm, golden sand
I can hear the silky blue, foaming sea
The latest 'top reads' all near me by hand
Back to the hotel, I search for the key

I sit on the bed, the room is all clean
Not a flip-flop or hat out of its place
Then I do realise the maid must have been
That is a job I know I couldn't face!

Strolling by the beach in the dark of night
It is so different than before
The magnificent moon is really bright
If only we could stay forever and more.

Shona Smith (12)
St Edmund Arrowsmith Catholic High School, Ashton-in-Makerfield

A Night Mystery

Standing alone in a field,
Gigantic trees surrounding,
The river is silent,
I feel alone,
Scared, yet excited,
There is a small figure in the velvet night sky,
I see it approaching me,
It moves swiftly,
Like a butterfly,
It becomes larger and larger,
Until . . .

Emma Gibson (11)
St Edmund Arrowsmith Catholic High School, Ashton-in-Makerfield

Friends

I am going to talk about my best friends,
First, there is Lauren Roche, my best mate,
Next, there is Catherine where our friendship will never end.
Also, there is Laura, Alex, Charlotte and Rosie Pate,
Shona and Jordan are next in line,
Milaina is cool and really funny too,
When we go out we always have a good time,
We always chat and that's one thing we do.
We're not all best mates, we sometimes fall out,
But our friendship remains the same,
Laughter and fun, that's what it is all about.
Staying best mates is our main aim,
So there are a few of my best mates,
But I'll have to go now, it's getting late!

Lauren O'Donnell (12)
St Edmund Arrowsmith Catholic High School, Ashton-in-Makerfield

Acting

A person who acts is called an actor,
Actors perform on a large, curtained stage,
They get directed by a director,
The one who acts best gets the biggest wage.

The orchestra performs the best music,
The actor and actresses sing sad songs,
The music becomes very, very quick,
Suddenly, the orchestra hits two gongs.

The actress loves her adorable dress,
Although the actor sees lots of humour,
The director shout, 'I think it's a mess!'
An actor comes on, dressed as a puma.

The actors and actresses learn their lines,
The production is written by Tom Pines.

Matthew Biggs (12)
St Edmund Arrowsmith Catholic High School, Ashton-in-Makerfield

My Poem

I want to go far and become a film star,
I'm going to be a winner, it's my destiny
And hopefully be noticed in my fancy car,
Where they'll all crowd around, just to see me.

Which one shall I pick, horror or romance?
No romance, it's definitely my thing,
I'll marry a footballer and together we shall dance,
Actually, I think I might do musicals, I really want to sing.

I'm still in school and love drama to bits,
I've just been in the school production play,
One day I'll hopefully make it to The Brits,
I'll make sure I go all the way.

I want to make my dream a reality,
I'm going to do this for my friends and family.

Laura Beattie (12)
St Edmund Arrowsmith Catholic High School, Ashton-in-Makerfield

I Love Shopping

I love to shop wherever I can,
A shop, the mall, I'm a really big fan.
I will search all day for a skirt or top
And my motto is, shop till you drop.

Diamonds and rubies in every store,
I buy them all and I still want more.
A great big whiff of the delicious meals,
There's no time for that, I need new heels.

The shops are closing, my receipts have no end,
Maybe that's because I just spend, spend, spend.
I arrive at home alone with my bags,
So bored, I sit down with one of my mags.

Rebecca Cox (12)
St Edmund Arrowsmith Catholic High School, Ashton-in-Makerfield

Summer

In the daylight I see brightly coloured flowers
And birds taking ice-cold showers
I go out with my friends to play
'Let's have a water fight,' is what they say.

In the dead of night, outside is cool
Just like a great big swimming pool
It's really hot on the next day
So see your shadow and run away.

But soon the summer will come to an end
And the freezing will drive you round the bend
Can't wait to be out with my friend
Because this time next year, it will be summer again.

Emma Foulkes (11)
St Edmund Arrowsmith Catholic High School, Ashton-in-Makerfield

Sweets

Sweets, sweets, sweets, sweets,
Different sized tasty treats,
Chocolate and sherbet lemons
Bonbons and boiled melons.

Pineapple chunks are really nice,
Myself, I prefer sugar than spice,
I also like Uncle Joe's
I love tubs of cookie dough.

Bars of Dairy Milk are really dreamy,
Galaxy is like, totally creamy,
In my spare time, I love to make,
Lots and lots of sponge cake!

I love them all, each different kind,
Every one in my own mind.

Rachel Pointon (11)
St Edmund Arrowsmith Catholic High School, Ashton-in-Makerfield

Lost

Blood dripping from his wound,
His loss of breath,
His total stillness,
Seconds from his death.

The bomb fell from the sky,
The warning too late,
My home, nothing but rubble,
Everything and everyone I loved, gone.

Velvet tears rolling down my cheeks,
Painful emptiness and shock,
My world shattered,
On May 16th.

Even though I am still alive,
Inside, I am dead,
Repeated nightmares,
Of my brother, lying dead.

Elizabeth Darbyshire (11)
St Edmund Arrowsmith Catholic High School, Ashton-in-Makerfield

Seasons

There are four different seasons
For four different times of the year.
Winter is one that comes near Christmas
It's windy and snowy.
Autumn is another when the leaves
Turn brown and different colours.
Spring is also another when we go out to play
And have lots of fun in the sun.
Summer is the last one when we have our ice cream
And play in the boiling sun
We'll knock for our friends and have lots of fun.

Samantha McMinn (11)
St Edmund Arrowsmith Catholic High School, Ashton-in-Makerfield

Cricket

Cricket is my favourite sport,
Hitting and shooting for big applause,
Bowling with a corky and hitting a wicket,
I really love playing cricket.

I am now going to mention,
Flintoff the legend,
He can bowl really fast,
With a capital dash.

Stars like Flintoff are good for cricket
If I played them
They would soon have my wicket.

Matthew Woods (11)
St Edmund Arrowsmith Catholic High School, Ashton-in-Makerfield

A Knife In The Dark

Sitting on my own, in the middle of the night,
On a bench under a street light.
Leaves bluster and cluster, together all in the street,
Wondering if there is someone to meet.
A chill runs up my spine,
As a tall figure moves towards me in a straight line.
I see a knife in the dark or maybe it's just a lark,
As it moves closer I feel petrified, I should maybe run away,
Or maybe I should stay, as I see the knife I scream for help,
I hate to say this, but this could be my last day.
I'm coming to the last minutes of my life
I feel as scared as a fly
I might be going to *die!*

Joe William Wigley (11)
St Edmund Arrowsmith Catholic High School, Ashton-in-Makerfield

Miners

Shuffling their feet on the gritty floor,
Intensely following each other down the pitch-black tunnels,
Sharp rocks scraping their skin, then a man shouted, 'Don't go!'
They felt like they were breathing through funnels,
Suddenly, there was a loud crash,
They all turned round, to see that big rocks had blocked the tunnels
They stared at each other and started to choke,
Then all the men stumbled to the floor with a croak,
All that was left were dead bodies on the floor
And all ten men were loyal,
But as you know, miners come and go.

Jade Greenhalgh (12)
St Edmund Arrowsmith Catholic High School, Ashton-in-Makerfield

The Rugby Match

The crowds go crazy in the stalls ,
The ball is off and flying down the pitch,
The crowd are loud, I am deafened by their calls,
This game makes many people rich.

The Warriors take the lead,
The conversion over the sticks,
The defence is shouted at because of their speed,
The Wigan team have brilliant kicks.

Oh no, they've scored,
The celebrations are on,
The crowd are getting bored,
Could Wigan be gone?

Wigan have lost again,
They've come to an end, unlucky for them.

Luke Barlow (12)
St Edmund Arrowsmith Catholic High School, Ashton-in-Makerfield

Back In 1066-1500

Dead bodies on the floor with no heads at all
Arrows is the air, no way we'll win
The king's body lays in the king's great hall
Our soldiers armour is made out of tin.

They have lost their general, no way we'll lose
All of our men are armed with shields and swords
When we will win, we will drink lots of booze
When we win, the prince will be a lord.

They will run away, 'Retreat!' they will say
We will win no matter what they do
This very day will be their Judgement Day
We will win, we will win, we will win over you!

Ben Halton (12)
St Edmund Arrowsmith Catholic High School, Ashton-in-Makerfield

Fireworks

As the roar of the dragon,
Lights start to appear,
Red, yellow, green,
I shake in fear.

The roar has ended,
Now out comes the flames,
The flame is now silver,
Now he's not playing games.

As the flame turns to stars
And start to disappear,
The dragon goes to sleep
And has to wait another year.

Charlotte Hilditch (11)
St Edmund Arrowsmith Catholic High School, Ashton-in-Makerfield

Midnight

The clock strikes twelve,
I'm all alone,
The windows are shut,
The doors are closed.

The room is silent,
The night seems long,
The curtain is moving,
I'm not alone.

The lightning comes,
The window breaks,
The thing rushes out,
It has escaped!

Kathryn Harrington (11)
St Edmund Arrowsmith Catholic High School, Ashton-in-Makerfield

Police Officers

Police are loaded, wealthy and wise,
The job they have, I'm not surprised,
You're crossing the road, they'll give you a lift,
They're always glad when they've finished a shift.

Police will help you, if they've got the time,
Otherwise, they're solving a crime,
It's a serious job, but you can have a joke,
Maybe a drink and a glass of Coke.

You get a call from Chief Officer Kirk,
You partied all night, then missed work,
Then he says that he's got proof,
That the previous night, you slept on the roof.

You've missed work, don't die of depression,
Don't drink at night and you'll learn your lesson,
You've got the sack, you silly little yob,
So go to the station and beg for your job!

Kate Connor (13)
St Edmund Arrowsmith Catholic High School, Ashton-in-Makerfield

Wigan Athletic In The Premier League

Wigan Athletic in the Premiership,
Going down is the bookies tip,
Will not win a game till Boxing Day,
Relegated two months before May.

But the Latics boys will avoid the drop,
Beating teams who are at the top,
Man U, Arsenal, name them all,
The Wiganers will stand up tall.

With De Zeeuw and Henchoz at the back,
The other teams strikers will not attack,
With Mike Pollit, who plays in net,
Who is not scared to get very wet.

Paul Jewell's our manager, he is the best,
Obviously better than all the rest,
He came from Merseyside and is so cool,
Because he has his own swimming pool!

Believe it now we're in the Prem,
We'll be better than you, even with ten men!
Good team spirit is the key,
That makes us so good at the JJB.

Sam Whyte (11)
St Edmund Arrowsmith Catholic High School, Ashton-in-Makerfield

A View From The Top

I can see my house from up here,
It looks so small and quaint.
Fields upon fields of green, lush grass,
With enormous trees swaying in the breeze.

I breathe in the fresh, clean air
And have never felt more alive.
I smile and look up to the blue sky above me,
I feel so free; I just want to stay here forever.

Helen Jones (11)
St Edmund Arrowsmith Catholic High School, Ashton-in-Makerfield

Friends

I have lots of different kinds of friends
Funny, cool, smiley, stupid and mad,
Hoping our friendships will never end,
Friends make me laugh when I am sad.

Jayde, Catherine, Leanne and Nichola,
Are my best friends forever,
I know friendships will come and go,
But the special ones will stay together.

Bowling, shopping, cinemas and sleepovers,
Are a few of our favourite things,
Hoping no one will get mad when the curlers overheat,
The light turns off as all of us sing.

The special ones will stay and light up the world
And so will our hair when it is curled!

Erin Jayne Hutson (12)
St Edmund Arrowsmith Catholic High School, Ashton-in-Makerfield

Snowball

My cat's really small,
Like a little hairball,
My cat's very nice,
It likes to eat mice.

My cat's not that big,
She doesn't like to dig,
When I stroked my little kitten, it was furry,
When I stroked my other kitten, it was purry.

I bought my kitten
And it had a mitten,
My little kitten likes to eat
Lots of lovely veg and meat.

Katie Chesworth (11)
St Edmund Arrowsmith Catholic High School, Ashton-in-Makerfield

Chocolate

The chocolate I eat,
Is so very sweet,
Chocolate I like is white,
But can be very light.
Do you dare,
To eat an éclair?
A chocolate Galaxy Ripple,
Makes my mouth dribble
The chocolate in my mouth is so milky,
The wrapper can be really silky.
The different chocolates in my tummy,
Makes it sound so very yummy.
You think of chocolate that is all creamy,
That's when you start to go dreamy.

Rebecca Waterworth (12)
St Edmund Arrowsmith Catholic High School, Ashton-in-Makerfield

Strange Things

Strange things are always weird,
But sometimes they are feared:
The mottled frog,
Sat in the popping bog,
The computer freak,
Is just like a geek,
The smelly mule,
Boys think is cool,
Grandma is soppy,
Her kisses are sloppy,
My teddy is podgy,
He feels very squidgy,
Laura is lazy
And also crazy,
Just some of those strange things.

Julia Molloy (11)
St Edmund Arrowsmith Catholic High School, Ashton-in-Makerfield

In My Garden

I sit on my garden bench,
This is what I see,
A beautiful, big garden
And a stinging bumblebee.

There's an azure blue pond,
Rippling in the breeze
And giant green things,
Which are often known as trees.

Beautiful colourful flowers,
Which have the most wonderful smell,
I watch the birds flutter by,
Over the wishing well.

I see lots of different wildlife,
One of which is a butterfly,
Symmetrical and multicoloured,
I just love to watch it fly.

Rachel Lever (11)
St Edmund Arrowsmith Catholic High School, Ashton-in-Makerfield

During The Night

Lying in bed beneath the sheets,
Outside the trees rustle softly.
I hear a gentle pad of footsteps,
Curious I sit up in bed.
I notice a shadow, big and black,
I watch in terror as it moves towards me.
I lie in bed, terrified at what I may see,
But suddenly the creature attacks.
It lashes out, but not with claws or teeth,
But a friendly dog lick!

Emily James (11)
St Edmund Arrowsmith Catholic High School, Ashton-in-Makerfield

My Best Friend Laura

This is a sonnet about my best friend,
She is the maddest person that I know,
She can sometimes drive me around the bend,
But she's always smiling and never low.

She thinks that Jon Wilkin is really fine,
But I will be Wigan until I die,
She tries to convert me all of the time
And she rubs it in when they score a try.

I still love her loads though; she's a big star,
We went to McFly and had a great night,
She is my favourite person by far,
But like most friends, we do have the odd fight.

I'd like to dedicate this to Laura
And tell her I'd do anything for her.

Leah Roberts (14)
St Edmund Arrowsmith Catholic High School, Ashton-in-Makerfield

Roller Coaster

I hold my heart,
As the ride starts.
I can't close my eyes,
It'll ruin the surprise.
Round the bend,
Whilst screaming next to my dear friend.
Upside down,
Going round and round.
Getting off the ride,
Clutching my side.

Laura Taylor (11)
St Edmund Arrowsmith Catholic High School, Ashton-in-Makerfield

Outside My Window

I sit and look out of my window,
Each and every day.
Watching people hurry past,
Everyone too busy to stay.

In winter it's cold and icy,
As I watch the falling snow.
People should be careful,
For every step will show.

In autumn the weather is pleasant,
The trees stand tall and bold.
Colours of red and yellow,
Mesmerise me as leaves fall.

In spring the trees blossom,
It's beautiful to see.
As every pretty flower is,
Visited by a bee.

People lie down in summer,
Everyone relaxes and daydreams.
As children playfully run around,
In the warm sun's beams.

Looking out of my window,
People run past, or walk.
Sometimes I hear them whisper,
Sometimes I hear them talk.

Hannah Lockey (12)
St Edmund Arrowsmith Catholic High School, Ashton-in-Makerfield

Sporting Leg-Ends

England win a penalty
Baggsied by Becks
He slips when he kicks
The pitch is a wreck.

Cricket training yesterday
The captain, Michael Vaughn
He was dropped for the Ashes
Because he gave a yawn.

Here's Tiger Woods
Putting for a win
When he wins the trophy
He'll put it in the bin.

Here's Jonny Wilkinson
Running for a try
When he got over the line
He got mud in his eye.

England's about to win the cup
Next is Freddie Flintoff
When he went to hit the ball
He missed because of a bad cough.

Connor Hitchen (11)
St Edmund Arrowsmith Catholic High School, Ashton-in-Makerfield

Winter

Winter is an old, dying man,
He is tired and fragile.
The cloak he wears is white and frosty,
His face is pale and ghostly.

Bethany Farrell (11)
St Edmund Arrowsmith Catholic High School, Ashton-in-Makerfield

TV

I like to lie on my couch made of leather,
Whilst listening to the lady explain the weather.
I like to watch X-Factor on the third channel
And watch the judges behind the panel.

I like to watch BBC
And listen to CBBC.
I like to watch all the programmes
And eat lots of cheese and ham.

Emmerdale and Coronation Street are on ITV3,
Coronation Street is the best soap for me.
I like to watch football on Sky One,
But I like to watch EastEnders on BBC1.

I like to watch sports,
When they are sponsored by Tote.

Katie Redford (11)
St Edmund Arrowsmith Catholic High School, Ashton-in-Makerfield

Frost

I dampen children's hopes of playing outside
I freeze the roads to make cars swerve
I latch onto trees and make them shiver and shake
I fog up windows to stop people seeing outside
I push people over as they walk down the street
I twinkle when the sun shines on me
I can appear and disappear when I want to
I send a shiver up your spine when you see me
I make sharp ice drops freeze on cars
I then slowly die as the sun gets angry
And becomes blazing hot!

Alex Fulton (11)
St Edmund Arrowsmith Catholic High School, Ashton-in-Makerfield

Frostbite

I start on a cold, clear night
I make their toes cold in bed
I creep!
I crawl!
I freeze the water
The children skate on my face
'I'm so cold'
That's what I make them whisper!
I make them trip!
I make them slip!
I melt
I become water, clear blue water
Until the next clear, crystal toe-biting night.

Lauren Elizabeth Peters (11)
St Edmund Arrowsmith Catholic High School, Ashton-in-Makerfield

The Power Of Fog

I am like a thick grey cloud
I make it hard for car drivers to drive on the roads
I cover up windows on houses and cars
I block out the view
I have a best friend and his name is Frost
I make noise fade a lot every time a noise is made
I make people think they're going blind
I make it look like night during the day
I make people get wet as they walk through me
I love being fog!

Thomas Bailey (11)
St Edmund Arrowsmith Catholic High School, Ashton-in-Makerfield

Fire!

I have a sudden burst of energy, feeling the need
To spread my way through the rooms of the house
I run speedily along the cold plastic wires leading to the telly
I grow and grow until I am colossal
I rise, eating my way through the painted, plastered ceilings
Reaching towards the people
I glow, causing the humans to cover their eyes
I consume people with my fuming rage
I soon become impossible to defeat
Spreading from object to object like a fox jumping for its prey
I suddenly see water and I am unable to halt quick enough
I am dying down, down, lower than the floorboards
I make my sizzling noise, alerting the people,
Telling them that my source is dying
I soon fail to defeat the water
And I am *dead!*

Stefani Trwoga (12)
St Edmund Arrowsmith Catholic High School, Ashton-in-Makerfield

Fire

I spark up from an electric cable
I catch onto a tree
I get hotter and hotter
I spread all around
I destroy anything in my way
I turn red, orange and yellow
I take my first victim from the campsite below
I see a lake
I panic and panic
I'm going to be defeated
I've gone.

Chloe Murphy (11)
St Edmund Arrowsmith Catholic High School, Ashton-in-Makerfield

He Fell To The Floor, Quickly Playing The Ball

He fell to the floor, quickly playing the ball
And the other team shouting set and in,
He took three strides straight at the brick wall,
Then the defender received a sin bin.

The ref blew up to our team's advantage
And play on the field stopped dead with the clock,
We all got psyched-up with fire and rage
And gave our player the bug dumb prop.

Our coach and parents, all cheering aloud
And shouting our names to us,
By now the spectators made a large crowd
And the clock continued without a fuss.

We ended the game with a hard-fought, good win
And led the team, up with heads and chin!

Kieran Edwards (14)
St Edmund Arrowsmith Catholic High School, Ashton-in-Makerfield

The Unwritten Sonnet

Here's a sonnet that's very hard to write,
Can't think of the next line, but never mind,
My friend Sam will help me to get it right,
Everyone's written theirs, I'm so behind,
Pen's on the paper, no words in my head,
Still under construction, don't read it out,
Just empty space and nothing to be said,
Don't even know what I'm writing about,
Oh! An idea just came into my head,
Should I write it or carry on thinking?
If I don't write it, I will be so dead,
Can't get my sentences to start linking,
My teacher comes over to where I'm sat,
A finished sonnet she's looking down at.

Katie Simpkin (14)
St Edmund Arrowsmith Catholic High School, Ashton-in-Makerfield

Friends

True friends are special - they are always there,
Wherever you are, they will be around,
Whatever the situation, friends care,
You should be glad of the friends you have found.

When with friends, you can always wear a smile,
It's both easy and hard to make friends anew,
Friends should be there forever, not a while,
It doesn't matter if your friends are few.

If your friends leave, you may feel sad,
Even far apart, it will be all right,
If you keep in touch, it won't be that bad,
Don't worry if they're not within your sight.

Even if you and your friends are far apart,
They will always have a place in your heart.

Erin McVitie (14)
St Edmund Arrowsmith Catholic High School, Ashton-in-Makerfield

Irish Dancing Sonnet

Standing up on the stage waiting to dance,
With nervous excitement my heart races,
My back straight, I smile and await my chance,
All eyes on me and so many faces.
The music begins and I point my toe,
Hoping I will remember the action,
Counting with the beats, then off I do go,
Glancing around at the crowd's reaction.
My dancing teacher's voice sounds in my head,
Stay on your toes! Don't drop your heels! Legs up!
Luckily I remember what she said
And then it's over without a hiccough.
The results are called; I stare into space,
But to my surprise, I have won first place!

Catherine Byrne (15)
St Edmund Arrowsmith Catholic High School, Ashton-in-Makerfield

Poverty Sonnet

No way out, nowhere to go, no one cares
No more food left or fresh water to drink
Illness is spreading, still more and more scares
Is there anyone out there? I can't think!
This heat is too much with other things too
Life is like a jigsaw, mine doesn't fit
No money, no home, no life, what to do?
Much to do, *can't* complain, no time to sit
Clouds are forming, water falling, rain comes
No more drought, water to drink, crops will grow!
Finally a glimmer of hope for mums
Dads, everyone saved, progress will be slow
A long way to go, it's not over yet
Try to move forward, so much to forget.

Emma Bartlett (14)
St Edmund Arrowsmith Catholic High School, Ashton-in-Makerfield

Wigan Athletic FC

We all hurry down to the JJB
PJ's lads in a Premiership derby
All eyes on the clock, games kicks off at three,
Mr Teale stays home playing with his Barbie!

Ref blows his whistle, fans begin to roar
Noise erupts over the away end
Jason's through on goal - he's certain to score
Everyone buys pies, with the money that they spend.

Half-time arrives, along with all the fuss
Players get half-time drinks, feeling fatigued
Fans sing, 'And are you gonna believe us?'
Shortened pause, 'We're gonna win the league!'

Ninety minutes gone, the fans know it's true
Wigan's staying up and the town's turning blue!

Michael Feeney (14)
St Edmund Arrowsmith Catholic High School, Ashton-in-Makerfield

Golf

I walk up nervously to the last tee
I get my driver from my golf caddie
I swing it hoping I don't hit a tree
And whack the ball onto the fairway gladly
It's time to chip the ball onto the green
I swing with a lob wedge, it goes quite high
I'm astounded, it's the best shot I've seen
I can't believe it's as easy as pie
I take out a putter from my golf bag
Ready to sink the putt on the last hole
But as I'm swinging my feelings do sag
As I can never gauge how much it will roll
I hit it; it glides like a hockey puck
And rolls and falls gently into the cup.

Joshua Cieslar (14)
St Edmund Arrowsmith Catholic High School, Ashton-in-Makerfield

Y10

School is a drag, it's quite depressing,
Things started to go bad in September,
I lost my bag and my shoes went missing,
Homework is bad, it's increased in number.

Lessons are boring, with so much coursework,
English, maths, geography, science, French and art,
Coursework in them all, that's a tonne of work,
It feels like I have been hit by a go-kart.

With so much homework, I can't get a break,
I'm up for hours every evening,
With stupid maths sums, it's too much to take,
If this keeps up, I might end up killing!

I've had enough, I want to go to bed,
After two years of this, I'll end up dead.

Andrew Price (14)
St Edmund Arrowsmith Catholic High School, Ashton-in-Makerfield

Wigan Athletic FC

Premiership has arrived and hopes were high
Jose's Chelsea first at the JJB
On the menu, a traditional pie,
Camara joined with a big transfer fee,
Charlton next and another one-nil loss,
Win against the Mackems, Lee Mac was fit,
Then West Brom, where Arry won the toss,
'Judas' did nothing as Jimmy won it,
Points against Boro and Everton too,
Big Sam's Bolton couldn't stop the good run,
Nothing Rodney can do, Wigan *is* blue,
And beating the Toon was a lot of fun,
Happy next May and forget Wigan pier,
Champions League will complete a great year!

James Whyte (14)
St Edmund Arrowsmith Catholic High School, Ashton-in-Makerfield

Think Of A Story That I Know Quite Well

Think of a story that I know quite well,
Change into a sonnet and win the prize,
Was stuck but I needed something to tell
And it all was blank in my mind's own eyes.

Rack my brain for a theme to write about,
Ask people for help, but to no avail,
Hear the others say, 'I can think of nowt!'
Can't think of a story, nor of a tale.

Then it hit me; I now know what to write,
Answers will come from my questions inside,
Use this as my sonnet to end my plight
And now all my troubles have long since died.

Thought of a story that I know quite well,
No longer stuck, I've got something to tell.

James Schorah (15)
St Edmund Arrowsmith Catholic High School, Ashton-in-Makerfield

Pets

Liam sews hats for his cats
Katie has a triumphant elephant
Rachel's lion like to iron
In the fog, Adam walks his dog
Nathan did plaits for his rats
Hannah digs food for her pigs
Amy's snake eats cake
And Laura's bat is very fat.

Hannah Miller (11)
St Edmund Arrowsmith Catholic High School, Ashton-in-Makerfield

Reality

Newborn babies cry without a smile,
Homeless people begging for food.
Fostered children going through a hard time,
Orphans waiting for their freedom, their new class family.
Celebrities running from the press, looking for their limo.
Criminals out to do the worst,
Teachers in school to teach,
The bullied unsafe and the bullies capable of the worst,
Firefighters putting out fires,
Police officers stopping crime,
Paramedics saving lives.
NSPCC helping abused children,
RSPCA helping abandoned animals,
Disabled people suffer, but still get around with a smile.
Judges at a court case trial,
Terrorists walk around with criminal minds,
The dead in their afterlife
Natural disasters cause emotional pain,
Law doesn't bother thugs,
Hidden talents of street dancers gets shown off on the streets,
Men, women and children in Africa die every day of AIDS!

Sofia Khan (13)
The Hollins Technology College

Sea Breeze

Shore of the sea with crashing waves,
Then retreating back in.
Boats going out of the harbour with another entering
Tall trees swaying in the breeze.
Sun beating down.
People entering the sea with others running out,
Hotel's on a mountaintop
Night falls and all wait for a new day to begin.

Jordan Lynch (13)
The Hollins Technology College

The Hollins

The Hollins is fun,
The Hollins is great,
It isn't a dump down the grate.
People at The Hollins are loud, exciting and fun,
But there's some who are quiet, peaceful and boring.
The teachers are strict but a little fun,
You won't get away with anything mad,
You will get punished so don't bother being bad!
The classrooms are colourful and good to learn in
We can drink water to help us learn but you're not allowed
To drink or eat anything else, but don't be fooled,
Nearly all the kids chew.
At dinner time at 1 o'clock we all line up to get into the canteen,
Apart from Year 11, they have the privilege just to walk in.
We eat our dinner like dogs that have been starved
For a number of weeks and then go out into the covered way.
At the end of the day, we can't wait to get out of school
And go out with our mates.
The Hollins is fun,
The Hollins is great,
The school buses are outside the school gate!

Bill Todd (13)
The Hollins Technology College

9Y1

First there's Christina Ainsworth, she is the new kid
Then there's Haroon Akbar, he is the mischievous one
Next there's Sara Bano, she has diabetes
Then there's Michael Bolton, he is the cool kid
Next there's Rebecca Buck, she's the fashion goddess of the class!
Then there's Joe Connor, he's the snooker player
Next there's Lauren Cunliffe, she's the holiday freak
Then there's Stacey Dewhurst, she's a group kind of girl
Next there's David Dickinson, he's an engineer
Then there's Jade Dodd, she is the small kid
Next there's Thomas Godfrey, he's the computer whizz-kid!
Then there's Ruby Iqbal, she is the glamour model
Next there's Samira Khan, she's the jewellery freak
Then there's Sofia Khan, she is the chatterbox
Next there's Jordan Lynch, he is my best friend
Then there's Nick Main, he is the American kid
Next there's Joshua Morris, he's the funny one
Then there's Shannon Moseley, she is loud and cheerful
Next there's me! Daniel Pitt, I am the Welsh boy!
Then there's Jay Riches, he's the footie star!
Next there's Rosie Rudge, she's the dancing queen
Then there's Bill Todd, he's the tall kid
Next there's Samantha Ward, she is the sweet and innocent one
There there's Sam White, he's the rugby star
Next there's Anne-Marie Whitehurst, she is the kind and shy one
Finally, there's Khawar Younis, he's the tough kid!

Daniel Pitt (13)
The Hollins Technology College

The Seasons

The lambs are born all white and fluffy like a cloud,
The children are playing on the new spring grass,
The trees have woken up.
The trees suddenly get their leaves back,
All golden, brown and green,
The hot sun is beating down,
Children playing and running around,
The dogs and owners sitting down,
Enjoying the long days ahead.
The strong breeze blowing the leaves,
Around and around on the grassy grounds,
The trees have been stripped bare with nothing to wear,
The children wearing coats, scarves and gloves
Even though the sun is out,
They are playing in the park,
Pretending to be sharks,
The water washing over the children, cooling them down,
The hot summer days have gone.
The ground is as white as a sheet,
Hoping people will walk on it,
The cold winter's wind blowing
While everybody is all wrapped up inside.
The children are playing games and looking forward to Christmas,
Opening their presents and carolling.
The people are looking forward to a brand new year.

Sara Bano (13)
The Hollins Technology College

Prancing Through The Park

The wind rustling
Through the trees
The shaking of
My freezing knees.

The squirrels running
From tree to ground
The little squeak
Of the squirrels' sound.

The sound of the children
Playing on the ground
So silent
You can't here a sound.

The gentle sound
Of the birds calling
The loud noise
Of the parents bawling.

The birds singing
Song to song
The days drag on
And feel so long.

Shannon Moseley (13)
The Hollins Technology College

Memory Poem

Mum and Dad said,
'We're going to Disneyland tomorrow.'

It's morning now
And we're ready to go in 5, 4, 3, 2, 1 . . . *boom!*
We're there now and all I want to do is explore,
Go on all the big rides with Dad,
Go to the shops with Mum
And eat lots of candyfloss!

Slap! We went to watch a show
To see delirious dolphins
Diving and jumping through hoops
With people on their backs!

Crack! We're all playing big banging
Booming and pinging instruments all day long!

Va va voom! I'm upside down
Swirling, swaying and slithering
All over the big rides with Dad!

Whip! I'm getting lots of shopping with Mum!

Sizzle! I'm at home in bed with Teddy!

Amber Connolly (11)
The Hollins Technology College

A Phase In Summer

Summer is fun
Because you get to play in the sun.

Summer can be boring
Because you have to go to school.

Summer is fun when you are outside
And not in boring school.

Summer is good, you can go swimming
And do things fun when you aren't in school.

Summer holidays are good because I help my dad
We do jobs for Blackburn with Darwen Council.

In summer the birds sing and the fish swim happily
Me and my mates go swimming in summer.

Summer, things to do:
Go bowling, go swimming, go playing outside.

That is the end of my poem about summer!

David Dickinson (13)
The Hollins Technology College

My Memory

The kick-off, all run to the ball
Running like a cheetah and battling like a lion
All to score that one goal.

Slipping, sliding, shooting, saving
He shoots, *bang!* But sadly hits the post.

Finally, one on one with the keeper
Boom! What a goal, the crowd go wild
And his teammates dive on him.

They're attacking with some pace here
The winger's got the ball
A great cross into the box
And a header towards goal.

Jamie Bates (11)
The Hollins Technology College

Missing You

I miss your smile
I miss your laugh
I miss the way you liked to act daft.

Your hair so long
Your hair so fair
Your hair so long it flew in the air.

Your comfort so good
Your confidence so tough
Your advice so good I couldn't get enough.

I miss you a lot
Each day even more
Life without you can be such a bore.

That one special person
That one special smile
That one person for that you would walk a mile.

Rosie Rudge (13)
The Hollins Technology College

Night

Night is when
The sun goes to sleep
And when the moon shines upon us.

Night is when
The trees play a game of dominos
And when the trees rustle like a herd of animals
When the owls play hide-and-seek
And when the letter boxes play
Chinese whispers.

Night is when
Everything is quiet
And stars appear.

Samira Khan (13)
The Hollins Technology College

Memory Poem

When I was younger I would wonder,
If I would become a nurse.
I would dress up as a nurse
And make my dolls look worse,
Then my mum would get her purse
And down to the shops we'd go
But by then, I had set another curse.

When I was younger I would wonder,
Was I to become a vet.
I once had my own pet,
A dog it was and I'd help it like a real vet.

So when I was younger I would wonder,
Was I to become a bus driver.
I'd make a bus and give out tickets
And that's how I made money.

When I was younger I would wonder,
What I would really be.
Maybe a nurse, or even worse
A bus driver,
When I was younger
I would wonder!

Abbie Coulthurst (11)
The Hollins Technology College

Memory Poem

Squelching, scattering, scratching,
Searching that's my hamster Harvey.
He's so seductive seeing him perform
Sensational scarcely seen moments,
His cuddly soft fur I could hug him like a teddy bear.
My hamster Harvey is not very tall
In fact he is very small
I am quite scared he might run into a wall
Or maybe worse, he might have a great big fall.

Fuming, fast, fascinating, fearful that's my kitty, Fluff
Poor Fluff she usually got all the attention
She thought to herself it was more like she had detention
It was in my best intentions to mention
My new addition to the family
But I forgot to ask Fluff about her opinion
Which was the biggest mistake I made of all.

As you can imagine, they were both full of resentment and hate
All I ever wanted was for them to get along
And be the best of mates!

Fluff stood outside the kitchen door
Waiting to see more of Harvey
Waiting, waiting, he sat in silence
Waiting for Harvey,
But Harvey never came because he was frightened
And cowered in his cage.

Nicola Hickey (12)
The Hollins Technology College

My Memory Poem!

In my mind and in my soul,
A memory started to unfold.
A true thing of what I have done,
A possibility greater than fun!

I looked after a dog,
Short and small.
Who barked and pounced,
Like a know-it-all.

Ruff! She barked, squirming around,
Quick, look out, she's ready to bound.
Crash! I heard, as I came in,
A little white dog stuck in a bin.

'Oh, where are you, you Silly Sally?
I'm coming to get you and I won't dilly-dally.'

I didn't want to say she was a bad girl
But then I felt a gigantic big whirl.

So please come here you predictable pup,
Now here's your food and please shut up!

Lee Caldecott (11)
The Hollins Technology College

Rugby

The whistle blows, the match will begin
We came to play, we came to win
This team we face are hard and good
It could end in tears or even blood
I ran so hard, my lungs ached
We're not here to lose so the pain I will take
I tackle hard, the ball I nick
Maybe I'll run or maybe I'll kick
The crowd cheer my brilliant try
The kick's converted with a cry.

Sam White (13)
The Hollins Technology College

My Class 9Y1

The class came in eating food
My teacher thought this was very rude
She got mad and the class was glad
Rosie R and Shannon M sat in their seats like very good friends.
Ann-Marie and Sara were very quiet and Jade too
People kept asking to go to the loo.
Khawar and Haroon were talking loud
And Miss looked like she was going to burst like a black cloud.
Mickey B was trying to listen to music but the class were OTT.
Most of the class were getting on with their work
And Miss Forbes started to squawk!
Saying, 'Be quiet!' and 'Chill out!'
And a big noise said, 'Bill, out!'
Everyone laughed and the bell rang
And the kids ran out and Miss Forbes sang for joy!

Samantha Ward (13)
The Hollins Technology College

Down In The Jungle

Down in the jungle
There are birds and mice.

Down in the jungle
There are flowers and flies.

Down in the jungle
There are trees and bees.

Down in the jungle
There are rabbits and fleas.

Down in the jungle
There are deer and bears.

Down in the jungle
All you can hear is *buzz* and *hiss.*

Down in the jungle
All you can see is trees and leaves.

Jade Dodd (13)
The Hollins Technology College

My Memory

Riding on the roller coasters
Really having fun
Cuddled up to my dad
Snug as a gun.

Messing with my sister
All day long
On the karaoke
Singing songs.

Having fun
Having a laugh
Going inside
To take a bath.

Going home from Turkey
Sad as can be
My mum and my dad
Comforting me.

Natalie Oldham (11)
The Hollins Technology College

Memory Poem

Starting school is scary
Especially for a four or five-year-old
I can remember it like yesterday.

Walking through the reception door
All I could hear was
Crash! Bang!
And people talking.

Later on we had to have horrid milk
And I hated it!
So I stood on it
Milk went flying everywhere and on everybody.

My mum said she was always good
But I am not going to follow people like that
I will be
Myself!
Well, it's the only person you can be!

Lauren Graham (11)
The Hollins Technology College

Memory Poem

Outside my bedroom a loud drilling sound
When the water comes out the pressure washer
My brother car washing I look down.

His strong, aching back comes up from the ground
Sponge in his hand wiping furiously
Happily wiping under the hot bright sun.

Spraying water on the car
Washing all the soap away
Then he stops for a cup of tea
And then continues working all day.

Waxing the car with his mighty hands
Making the car really shiny
Then he gets in the car and parks it under the shining sun.

Between my fingers and my thumb
A calculator rests
I'll wash with it.

Akbar Hussain (11)
The Hollins Technology College

Memory Poem

When I was nine I went to Disneyland, Paris
I can remember it off by heart,
Planning what time to get up,
What to wear
And how I would go to bed early
But when the night came
I couldn't sleep,
I was up and down every minute
When Mum told me to go to sleep
So I did, I drifted off into a deep, deep sleep
When suddenly *beep, beep*
The alarm clock was off, the journey began.
Coming downstairs was my brother looking very tired
He wasn't even excited he was too young
Grandma and Grandad took us to the airport
After two hours we boarded the plane
Up and up, high in the sky.

Hannah Fawcett (11)
The Hollins Technology College

Memory Poem

Walking through the school doors
All I saw was groups of fours
People shouting calling names
People playing football games.

When I went into my form
I was scared and went all warm
Until the teacher welcomed us
As you will love it here
So I believed her, she was great
Just as great as my mate.

When the day got near the end
The last class I went to
Was English with my friend.

I won't forget
My first day at school
I loved it
It was really cool!

Hannah Pritchard (11)
The Hollins Technology College

Tree

Playing innocently by its roots,
We were drawn towards it.
Branches reaching up, up and out of sight;
Like a ladder up to the clouds.
Huge leaves, as big as, bigger in fact, than hands.

This, we thought, was made to climb
Yet there were no branches low enough to reach.
So we just sat and thought for a while
And thought . . . and thought . . . and thought some more.
Yet no brilliant ideas came, no stroke of genius.
This, my friend said, was too much of a challenge
And just as he was about to go away.

I was struck by inspiration and stood in a bush nearby
My friend stared
I climbed up to its highest branch and then,
Without thinking, leapt for the tree.

Scrambling, struggling and slipping
I hauled myself up onto a branch, yes! Oh yes!
I had done it! I had climbed it!
The biggest tree in the land!
And then I slipped and fell back into a bush!

Rachel Butterworth (11)
The Hollins Technology College

My Memory Poem

It was a Saturday morning
I was really excited I was going
To Camelot theme park.

We were in the car I was so excited
I just couldn't wait
Half an hour later we were there
I saw the ride I was planning to go on
It was huge.

I ran towards it,
Then I saw how fast it went.
I had never been on it before
My heart started beating so fast
I didn't want to go on it anymore.

I did go on it though, because my cousin forced me
I was in my seat, the ride started
I had a funny feeling in my stomach
We were near the top now
We went down, it was going so fast
The wind was in my face, but I wasn't scared
I was enjoying the ride!

Saif Hussain (11)
The Hollins Technology College

Memory Poem

Upset, I walked up the steep hill,
Legs like jelly, but I just kept on walking,
Walking past rocks, past rocks and trees.

Shouts in my head, I just had to get away,
Rowing and roaring at each other,
I was scared, they weren't Mum and Dad,
They were more like evil clones on a battlefield.

There was a stile in the fence by the side of me
I climbed over and looked at the view,
Caravans and tents scattered like wild flowers,
Such a sad moment for such a beautiful view.

It was still too early to go back,
They were probably ripping the caravan to pieces
And along with it, each other.

I climbed higher and higher,
Telephone lines above,
Away from the view now,
Trees around but there's an opening ahead.

The view up here is wonderful,
I'm really high,
I can see a lake, the campsite and the village,
It's now time to go back.

Matthew Gregson (11)
The Hollins Technology College

Memory Poem

At the tips of my toes
The football rests.

Running, passing, shooting, *goal!*
A beastly shot soaring through the air
Like an eagle.

Swooping towards the goal
Twisting and turning
Like a theme park ride.

And it's . . . saved, *oh no!*
Maybe next time.

It tees up again
I swing my leg as hard
As a big Bertha golf club.

It's going, going . . . *goal!*
A crowd of players dashing towards me
Like a pack of lions.

At the tips of my toes
The football rests,
I'll score with it.

Joshua Bray (11)
The Hollins Technology College

Memory Poem

As I get out of the car
My foot lands on the black concrete
This is where my day begins
I look up, holding one hand on the car and fall back down
Those who go on these rides are so brave
These rides aren't suitable for me; I'm too petrified.

I walk to the rides, the terror is getting closer
My target, my challenge
Is to place myself on the hot seat of a roller coaster
I'm as scared as a mouse
But those who are scared, aren't as scared as me
These rides aren't suitable for me; I'm too petrified.

I sit on it, it's the best day of my life
I can't let myself and my family down
It goes up and down
As fast as the wind of a hurricane
I couldn't talk, the wind was trapping my voice
The ride stopped, I looked down
I couldn't believe it, I sat on a roller coaster
These rides *are* suitable for me, I'm *not* too petrified!

Amelia Iqbal (11)
The Hollins Technology College

Memory Poem

On my foot
The football lies, itching to go, like me,
The ground slippy, soggy, muddy
Our ref blows his whistle,
We kick off.

We dodge through the other team,
I am a defender
We tackle the other team and get the ball,
Cross it in and score a goal!

Next two matches fly by
With two easy 2-0 wins.

The final's come along
A much harder game for us,
Some touch tackling is going on,
Our team is fowled
We get a free kick
Our captain steps up to take it
We score a goal and win the competition!

Between my finger and my thumb
The gold medal rests
As proud as can be!

Amy Jenkinson (12)
The Hollins Technology College

Memory Poem

In front of me a building
A building with lots of floors,
I stand in the middle
In the middle of two big doors.

First we had assembly
We went to the main hall,
The teacher talked on and on
When we had an emergency call.

The fire bell rang loud and clear
And we filed into the tennis court,
At the start of the day the teacher told us what to do
And we all did everything we had been taught.

After that, we had our dinner
We queued up for fish and chips,
Then we had our music lesson
Where we played till we had sore lips.

Our teacher went all moody
And her face was fiery red
'Will you behave!' she cried
Before fainting and banging her head!

Well, this is where my day ends
So you can go and get a cup of tea
And I'll go out to Ben's.

Iram Akhtar (11)
The Hollins Technology College

Memory Poem

Pancake Day, *yum-yum*
Whipped cream and strawberries in my tum
I couldn't wait
Till my brothers went to school.

I sat down with a big grin
From ear to ear down to my chin
My mum goes up and I look down
At the fishes with an idea . . .

I'd give her a surprise, to brighten up her day
Slipping, sliding
Running and gliding, *crash, bang, wallop*
It was ready.

As she came down
She had a massive frown
That spread all over her face.

The fish tank was grey
All whipped cream squirted to the bottom
I tried to feed them
I guess it didn't work!

My mum had to fish them out
I could see she wasn't too happy
She's such a bore!
I don't understand, I'm only four!

Shahana Begum Ali (11)
The Hollins Technology College

My Memory Poem

I wake up in the morning
And squeeze my stomach tight
It's my first day at high school
And I can't bear the big fights.

'You'll get your head flushed down the toilets!'
'You'll get bullied by everyone!'
'You'll get such hard work, no matter what!'
But Mum just says they're joking!

But when Mum comes downstairs with me
That feeling fades away
My mum is so great, I'm telling you
She reassures me that it's going to be OK.

Bang!
The time has come and I'm in the school
Mum was right, it's brilliant!
'I can't wait for tomorrow,' I say
As I head for home.

I laugh out loud to myself
I can't believe what I was told!
'They're all big *fibs!*' I say
As I give a huge sigh of relief!

Mehreen Arif (11)
The Hollins Technology College

Memory Poem

Sitting on the rides,
Going higher and higher,
Cool breeze wafting on my face,
People having fun.

Popcorn being eaten,
Ice cream being licked,
People win teddy bears
And lots of other gifts.

Banging into cars,
Going round and round,
Getting wet on the log flume
And drying in the sun.

Spooky sound here and there,
People enjoying the day,
Faces being painted,
Cats, monkeys and a little bear.

Hundreds of tired people,
Rubbing eyes and yawning,
Time to go home,
Belt-up and off we go.

It's morning,
I wake up,
It was a dream
Of my day at Camelot!

Naiela Qureshi (12)
The Hollins Technology College

My Memory Poem!

Bang! Crash! Hiss!
Money has been lost,
The workers are trying to persuade me to have another game
It's like I'm in the market square and they are echoing at me.

Under the Galleon the wind blew it up even higher
So it began to rock even faster side to side,
The Galleon was high in the sky, when I realised
There was nowhere to go
It banged in the trees and got trapped in the bark.
It wouldn't come out, everyone was terrified of the tragic incident
The Galleon controller was shocked.

The Galleon was scattered from the end
The anchor and the paint landed on the floor with a *bang!*
It was nowhere to be seen.

Nazia Ilyas (11)
The Hollins Technology College

Memory Poem

I put the hat on my head
I put the boots on my feet
I saddle up and grab the reins
I am ready.

Between my fingers and my thumb
The reins lie gently as snug as a gun.

The *clip-clop, clip-clop* of the horse's four hooves
Scraping along the ground.

Trotting along, the feeling of doing something
For the first time
How marvellous.

Between my fingers and my thumb
The reins lie gently as snug as a gun.

David Ferenc (11)
The Hollins Technology College

On The 31st October

On the 31st of October
When it is dark
And every is out
Trick or treating at Dovdale Park.

A cold, windy night
That may give sane children a fright
Witches on broomsticks
Swap silly scares for candy sticks
Scared and excited
Laughing, screaming, thunder and lightning.

Rain lashing down
Spine shivering and quivering
Hand to hand with each other
Sisters and brothers
Watched over by ghouls riding lush in the sky.

Adam
Tulketh Community Sports College

Hallowe'en

Hallowe'en is once a year
And is meant to fill people with fear
Spooky ghosts, vampires and bats
And witches who wear pointy hats.

Children like to play trick or treat
And bobbing for apples which they like to eat
They cut faces in a pumpkin head
And insert a candle so light will be shed.

Although it is a scary night
And you might see a spooky sight.

It's still good fun
On October 31!

Charmaine Dean (14)
Tulketh Community Sports College

Hallowe'en Night

Scary Hallowe'en night,
Freaky costumes made to fright.
Witches, wizards, all kinds of ghouls,
The kind we only write about at school.

Vampires with razor teeth,
Devouring neck like juicy roast beef.
Bats flying through the air,
It just gives people a scare.

One night a year, when the spooks call,
The creepiest night of them all!

Dean Ross (12)
Tulketh Community Sports College

Hallowe'en Fright

One terrible Hallowe'en night
There were shadows coming from the woods
Dark red blood was splattered all over
Disturbing screams could be heard from the centre of the woods
Gross green slime was all over the floor
All of a sudden a bloodthirsty beast leaped out
I ran for my life, scared as hell
The beast had jet-black eyes
Stunk like a rotting corpse
It had fangs as sharp as Samurai swords
Bigger than my head
I leapt out of its way
And landed in my Hallowe'en bed!

Anthony Fisher (11)
Tulketh Community Sports College

In The Cemetery

In the cemetery,
Late at night,
Goblins,
Ghouls
And ghosties!

Tonight is the night,
They will give us a fright,
We will go out till late tonight,
Prepared for a fight!

Straight to my neck,
The vampire's sharp bite!
Bats fly through the sky,
Maybe someone will die,
Thunder and lightning,
Thumps and bumps,
All through the night!
Sounds of fear and fright
All through the night!
A foul stench in the air,
Knocking on Death's door,
Dripping blood on the floor,
Black cloaks hiding,
Sharp teeth biting,
Hallowe'en night goes on!

Nathan Oldham (11)
Tulketh Community Sports College

The Light Goes Down

The light goes down,
The sound of bone crunches lingers around,
The buried bodies shake the ground.
People stop and see ripped and bloody gowns,
Screams and shouts as the zombies take the town.

The light goes down,
No one makes a sound . . .
Scream is here,
He'll make more than a tear,
More than fear,
People run far and near,
Creatures die, humans die.

The light goes down,
Chuckie is here,
He'll chop off your ear,
When he senses your fear,
People die, people cry and people sigh.

The light goes down
Carl is here
The dragging of chains
Scent of ogres' old drains
Sharp teeth like daggers
Slice into your flesh
The Schmitz monster loves
The taste of a warm neck!

Carl Szmit (11)
Tulketh Community Sports College

Teachers

Some teachers are nasty,
Some are super great,
Some can be iffy,
Some can be your mate.
Some look smart,
Some look untidy,
Some can be sound,
Some can be snidy.
Detentions you get,
If you are bad,
The only teachers that give you them,
Are the ones that are mad.
At the start of the day,
Teaching is what they want to do,
At the end of the day,
Some want ciggies and some want a brew.
So that's enough of taking the mick,
Because if I mention the word teachers again
I think I will be sick!

Garry Longshaw (12)
Tulketh Community Sports College

Scary Hallowe'en

Pumpkin heads moving,
Doors creaking in the wind.
Rats running across the room,
Rubbing.
Screams from another room,
Footprints on the floor.
Blood and bones up the unstable stairs
The TV is too loud
The horror film racing
Hallowe'en night and dark thoughts rampaging.

Adam Cross (11)
Tulketh Community Sports College

Bad Dream!

Screaming, shouting all around,
Creepy-crawlies on the ground,
Dressing up,
Trick or treat?
Spiders hanging from a tree,
I really, really want to scream!
I can see the moonlight's beam,
Walking slowly, being quiet,
I can't see anybody in sight,
Then . . .
Boo!
I run away and scream,
I look behind me,
Nobody there,
I trip up, footsteps coming closer
Then I wake up,
I look out of my window,
Red glowing eyes,
Give me a fright,
The day before Hallowe'en night!

Rebecca Whewell (11)
Tulketh Community Sports College

Hallowe'en

Wolves and ghouls will kill you,
So beware of what lies there,
Be careful what you're doing,
Because you might just get a scare.

Rats and mice will bite you,
So be careful where you go,
Knock on the door, say trick or treat
And see what lies in store.

Charlotte Carroll (12)
Tulketh Community Sports College

Trick Or Treat?

Screaming and shouting,
Masks on faces,
People dressed up,
For a night of their vision,
Tricking and treating,
All the candy you can eat,
Vampires,
Werewolves,
Witches and devils,
Wind and rain,
Cold and snowy,
Wet and damp,
Scaring you with a jolt!

Samantha Cowley (11)
Tulketh Community Sports College

Doomsday

Darkly circling the Doomsday wood,
Night closed over the world.
Shadows rose from beneath the ground,
Ghouls and goblins danced cruelly around.

Vile, monstrous teeth,
Like razor-sharp spikes,
Preparing to slice warm flesh.

Rusty jagged claws,
To scratch at the ground
And penetrate soft cheeks.

Snapping necks like candy sticks,
This is how ghosts get their kicks.
On Hallowe'en night there are only tricks.

Chris Hurles (13)
Tulketh Community Sports College

Watch Out, Hallowe'en's About

So spooky, so freaky,
All the costumes I can see,
It's scary, it's creepy,
It all really frightens me.

Children trick or treating,
Ghouls, ghosts, witches, all around,
Watching children eating,
The candy they have found.

I'm really scared right now,
Everyone is scaring me,
Someone's dressed like a cow,
Argh! Please help! Can't you see?

Yesterday was scary,
I'm so glad there's no more,
People said, 'Scary Mary!'
It was all really a bore!

Terri-Anne Duffy (11)
Tulketh Community Sports College

Hallowe'en

Trick or treat?
Something to eat,
A penny or two,
Or I might scare you!

Witches and cats,
Rats and bats,
A ghost or two,
Might scare you!

Rats and bats,
Wolves and ghouls,
Have all scared you!

Hayley Duckworth (11)
Tulketh Community Sports College

Hallowe'en Night

No moon in the sky,
Pitch-black at night,
Ghouls, ghosts, werewolves and vampires too,
Howling and screaming till their noise deafens you.

Nightmares creep into children's minds,
Just like a ghost coming to find
Something to scare.

Pumpkins with their freaky eyes,
Lit up, staring, staring . . .
Bats fly overhead,
Small children, buckets of sweets in hand,
Red eyes gleam in the dark,
Witches' cackles, bubbling cauldron, creaky door,
Ccccrrreeeeaak!
What's coming to get you?

Tosca Gunn (11)
Tulketh Community Sports College

Football Mad

Football is my game, I play it till I strain,
Wake up every morning and feel like I have a football brain.
Dad's going crackers 'cause I asked him for a game
Even though I love it, I'm not down in shame.
Loving it loads, loving it crazy
Hit the bar last week, but I scored a cracker today.
Dad said, 'You want a game?'
But me and Wayne hit a window on Walker Lane
And now I am in pain
And now I can't play my game.

Daniel Capstick (12)
Tulketh Community Sports College

Trick Or Treat?

Running door to door
Getting lots of treats
Like coins and sweets.

Stomach rumbling
Getting ready to eat
Feel like I'm running at a beat.

Dressed in black
Wearing a hat
Pointy nose
Evil eyes
Icy shiver down your spine.

And then . . .

Megan Brindle (11)
Tulketh Community Sports College

Hallowe'en Night

The door creaked but no one spoke
The door slammed to the hard, chipped wall.
Suddenly, a scream from the distance
Made my belly turn.
Silence struck the basement
There were small footsteps coming towards me.
I could hear the floorboards creaking
It was a small, black-cloaked women with a knife,
She ran towards me
It was a witch.
Oww!

Ebony Hamilton (11)
Tulketh Community Sports College

Hallowe'en

Wizard, witches, devils too,
All coming to get you.
Ghosts and ghouls, wild and free,
Hiding behind each hedge and tree.

Take a step outside,
It's worse than any ghost ride.
Say these words, 'Trick or treat?'
And you'll be the next meat they eat.

Life is over, life is gone,
When you meet a certain one.
He's green and scary, spiky too
And makes the sound, *tu-whit tu-whoo!*

So never try and stop him,
Or his girlfriend, Kim.
He'll take you down
With a frown,
Him and his brother, Tim.

Chevon Symone Green (11)
Tulketh Community Sports College

Hallowe'en

I went to a Hallowe'en party,
It was scary and alright.
It got trashed by ghosts,
In the middle of the night.

Me and my friends out in the dark
It is 12 o'clock at night
And the swings are moving in the park
What is this big light?
A witch comes out and gives us a big fright.

Boo!

Jordan Murray (11)
Tulketh Community Sports College

Sonnet

It is the power of the human race,
The ball hitting the corner of the net,
Yet brings racism which is a disgrace,
You win or you lose, then the score is set.

This is football, it's all glamour and fame,
You sit and you watch your favourite team,
They score, you shout, 'Go on lads, win the game!'
To win the Champions League is your dream.

It is by far the bestest ever sport,
Players like Frank Lampard and Ashley Cole,
But I wonder if I could play, I thought,
I could be striker and score super goals.

An after-match fight, we call it a brawl,
But this is my life and this is football.

Jamie Roberts (12)
Tulketh Community Sports College

Missing You

You will be missed by all and always in our hearts,
We will always be together, never torn apart
And now you are an angel, way up in the sky
And one day we will be together, with our wings, we'll fly.
Even though you're gone, I count you as a friend,
Nothing comes between us, our friendship never ends,
Every day I think of you, we'll always be together,
My love combined with your love, will go on forever.
The short time you were with us, was always full of love,
Goodbye for now, goodnight, God bless
From here to Heaven above.

Rebecca Michele Tyson (12)
Tulketh Community Sports College

The Night

High in the sky, there is the moon,
Midnight will be coming soon,
The moon's accompanied by the stars that shine,
The entire world feels like mine,
I feel like I am all alone,
All by myself, I feel unknown,
Shadows are crawling around my room,
Terrible dreams of doom and gloom,
I lay awake in the still of night,
The world around, consumed with fright,
All the ghosts begin to haunt
And creatures of the night laugh and taunt,
My little brother, sleeping tight,
No disturbances for him tonight,
Time seems to be standing still,
The night is keeping me against my will,
I wish I just could get some sleep,
Slumber silently without a peep,
Let me sleep silently in my bed,
Go away evil voices in my head,
Dark shadows behind my door,
Echoes of a tortured mind, screaming, 'Please, no more!'
In the night's darkest mist,
All the ghouls do exist,
Now that I have got some rest,
The night now thinks of its next test.

Megan Blackburn (12)
Tulketh Community Sports College

Spooky

Witch's nose,
Vampire's cape,
Cat claws,
In your face.

White sheets,
Scare you most,
Ghosts lurking through the night.

Witches' noses,
Big and pointy,
Festering wildly.

Vampire's cape,
Flowing around,
Like bats' wings above the ground.

Cats' claws,
Long and pointy,
Sharp as knives,
Scratching cruelly.

Skeleton's bones,
Crunching alone,
Creeps through the night.

Pumpkins lurking in the trees
Glowing orange and yellow
I don't feel so mellow.

Laura Bradley (11)
Tulketh Community Sports College

Night-Night

Creatures creep
While humans sleep
Night-night.

They try not to wake
As the trees shiver and shake
Night-night.

Everywhere they lay
All night, but never day
Night-night.

They never see the light
So they snuggle up tight.

Night-night creatures
Sleep tight!

Rebecca Mossop (12)
Tulketh Community Sports College

Hallowe'en Night

Hallowe'en night is always a fright
The witch, the cauldron and cats
Turn people into rats.
The night's moon like a glowing balloon
Outside a ghostly ride.
Masks and sweets all over the floor
Hallowe'en night, please no more!
In the castle, dungeon deep
Monsters creep.
You'll see them all
Dancing away at the monster ball.

Laura Roscoe (11)
Tulketh Community Sports College

The Magic Box

(Based on 'Magic Box' by Kit Wright)

I will put in the box . . .
The sound of the beach swishing away
The sweet perfume of a fresh red rose
People dancing in the cool waterfall.

I will put in the box . . .
The exotic feeling we all wish to have
Eagerness and enjoyment in something we don't know
The happiness from families.

I will put in the box . . .
A wish of desire
Relax in the yellow, perfect sunshine
Without lotion and have a beautiful burn-free tan.

I will put in the box . . .
Natural love
The feeling of love
The sound of love.

I will put in the box . . .
The texture of a baby's bottom
A baby's first smile
Cleverness from around the world.

Tasneem Abbas (12)
Walshaw High School

Love

Love is pink like fluffy candyfloss
It tastes like strawberries and cream
And smells sweet like freshly baked fairy cakes
It looks beautiful like a summer sunset
It sounds like the splashing waves on a Hawaiian beach
It feels like a butterfly fluttering inside you.

Zoe Marsden (13)
Walshaw High School

A Box Of Memories

(Based on 'Magic Box' by Kit Wright)

I will put in my box . . .
The first blossom on a tree
The last drop of the April showers
The pale light from the spring morn.

I will put in my box . . .
The crunch of a leaf under my foot
The first bonfire in the sky
The rich colours of autumn.

I will put in my box . . .
The first word of a baby
A Christmas tree in a garden
The first snowy day of winter.

I will put in my box . . .
A drop of the purest water from Arabia
A cocoon hatching into a butterfly
A bird's first flight.

I will put in my box . . .
A child's first snowman
The excitement on the eve of Eid
The laughter of my old grandma.

I will put in my box . . .
A green sky and blue grass
A boat on the open road
A racing car speeding down the sea.

I will decorate my box with . . .
The Northern Lights of Alaska
The fading colours of the rainbow
The brightest star from the sky.

And with my magic box I will . . .
Travel the seven skies
And make a home in Heaven
Then treasure my box forever.

Maria Hassan (13)
Walshaw High School

The Magic Box

(Based on 'Magic Box' by Kit Wright)

I will put in the box . . .
The windy black night,
The smell of the bonfire,
The smell of roses.

I will put in the box . . .
The ticking of the clock,
The screeching of the chalk board,
The flushing of the toilet.

I will put in the box . . .
The soft feel of velvet,
The smooth feel of a baby's bottom,
The rough scales of a crocodile.

I will put in the box . . .
Tasty chips and pizza,
Fizzy Coke and orange,
Colourful sweets and scrumptious chocolate.

I will put in the box . . .
The colours of the rainbow,
The sun shining over us,
The blue sky on a hot summer's day.

I will put in the box . . .
A girl on a broom, flying to the moon,
A cat flying with its ears as the wings,
A tiger and a giraffe shaking hands.

I will put in the box . . .
Red hot lava flowing out of volcanoes,
Water flowing gently down the river,
Huge mountains covered with blankets of snow.

Aisha Rashid (12)
Walshaw High School

My Good Friend!

Aneeqa brightens the day on a winter's morning
She laughs so much and makes me laugh too
She is so much fun
And she shines like the sun.
Aneeqa, Aneeqa, Aneeqa.
She makes me feel up when I'm down
She shines like the moon and the stars
She is so cool
She likes dancing in the pool
Aneeqa, Aneeqa, Aneeqa.
Aneeqa has hazel eyes
She is always being told to do her tie
But when I need help
She is there for me
Aneeqa, Aneeqa, Aneeqa.
She is a good friend!

Zara Ashraf (13)
Walshaw High School

People Say . . .

People say I'm annoying . . .
But I'm not.
People say I'm dumb . . .
But I'm not.
People say I am quiet . . .
But really I'm not.
Now when people say I'm clever . . .
That's something different
When people say I'm creative . . .
That's something different.
Now when people say I'm nice . . .
I just take it as a compliment and agree
That they are something different!

Saira Rafiq (14)
Walshaw High School

Dream, Night Or Day

Lightning arrowed across the sky,
Thunder clapped its mighty hands.
Darkness and fear swept the Earth,
Deserts, fire, water and land.

Gingerly, tenderly I walked across,
Craving for my destination.
My senses told me I was in trouble,
It's creeping up - this infestation.

Lightning arrowed across the sky,
Thunder clapped its mighty hands.
Darkness and fear swept the Earth,
Deserts, fire, water and land.

Propelling forward, spiralling down,
Deep, deep in this slumber.
The Caribbean, Bahamas,
People doing the rumba.

Then, *whoosh, bang, crack!*
Fear plates my face.
No sign of this loathing fear,
No clues, no evidence, not a trace.

This lightning, this thunder,
Branded across the sky.
No planes will fly across it,
No birds will fly.

All this poem is about,
What it's trying to say.
Is that the storm takes on many shapes,
Whether it's a dream, night or day.

Tahima Ali (13)
Walshaw High School

Bonfire - Haiku

The smell of bonfires
Late at night. But now there comes
The fierce, bright fireworks.

Amy Dewhurst (12)
Walshaw High School

I'm A Victim Of Crime

I'm a victim of crime
I've lived with it all of my life
I've been beaten and whipped
My mother just flipped
That's me; a victim of crime.

She left me at home on my own
Seven years old and so alone
With nobody to tell or to turn to
That's me; beaten till black and blue.

She takes it all out on me
I've done nothing wrong but turned on the TV
It's up to five times a day that she beats me
That's me; treated like a flea.

On my birthday, nothing for me
But a bit of a bun and a house key
I don't go to school anymore
That's me, that's me; not allowed out the door.

I have no friends because of Mum
I get bullied and have no fun
I always try and run away
That's me; the girl always in pain
That's me; the girl who has no brain
That's me; I'm neglected.

Sian Chadwick (14)
Walshaw High School

Fireworks - Haiku

Loud and colourful
All different shapes and sizes . . .
Bonfire Night is here!

Safia Anwar (13)
Walshaw High School

Weird Dreams

Weird dreams, what do they mean?
Have no idea, woke up with a scream
Was it comedy or scary?
People you don't know
Places where you don't go
End up in your sleep.
Things you've never seen before
Turn out in your weird dreams
Is it trying to tell you something?
Is it someone who's passed away?
Who do you see in your dream?
Do they smile or do they cry?

Or is it a dream where you die?
Maybe a dream of the afterlife
Do you wake up, look around and think
Was it real?
Or do you go back to sleep
Thinking it was just a dream?
Do you dream a weird dream over and over again
Or does this weird dream happen in real life?
When you know you're not asleep
When you know it's not a dream.

What does it mean to have a weird dream?

Saira Khan (13)
Walshaw High School

Unknown Beauty

As I gaze into the shimmering water
And see my reflection looking back at me,
Whilst the water boatman strides across,
Leaving streaks of glistening silver behind,
Mystifying me with its mesmerising beauty,
I sit there amazed at how the pond's charisma plays with my mind.

As I lift a stone and throw it into the silk-like water,
I see pearl ripples forming rapidly,
The wooden bridge arches over me,
Shielding me from the world around,
Protecting me from all the war and bloodshed.

I then realise how beautiful nature is,
How beautiful it could be
If only everyone could remove their invisible blindfolds
And notice Mother Nature's reality,
If only we thought about the advantages
Rather then the disadvantages
And didn't even think of playing with fate.

I'd live in this place of unknown beauty,
Rather than that place with its beauty known
But still ignored.

Kiran Iqbal (14)
Walshaw High School

Friendship

F ull of things to share with each other
a R e always there for each other
l I ke each other to death
n E ver let each other down
e N joy every minute together
a D dicted to each other
a S ure each other of our goodness.

Friends are forever!

Abeer Ejaz Butt (13)
Walshaw High School

Friend Or Foe?

I sit and wait for my life to be over,
As I wish and hope upon a clover.
If only I was born to a different life,
Never to see a beaten wife.
An innocent wall covered in tea leaves,
Never again to roll up his sleeve.
A punch or bang is all that it takes,
As his anger bubbles and bakes.
Daylight is a luxury that will soon be no more,
As I wish and hope he'd get out of that door.
In a coffin or in a box,
I sit and listen as that door locks.
He decides how far he will go,
Why does he treat me like a foe?

Giorgia Smithies (14)
Walshaw High School

Earthquakes

It happened in the morning
When the ceilings came down storming
People got stuck underneath
And now are covered with bandages and sheets.

Children are now orphans
People ringing ambulances on their phones.

It happened when the ground was shaken
Most lives were taken
The earthquake left behind
People with scarred minds
So please think about it
Some families are lucky they survived.

But we are more lucky
We weren't there!

Sanah Azhar (12)
Walshaw High School

My Trinket Box

(Based on 'Magic Box' by Kit Wright)

I will put in my box . . .
Boats in the sky floating, stars in the sea sinking
The sparkling shimmers of a sapphire and a ruby
The fizzy fizz pop melting and bursting on my tongue.

The delicious smell of traditional food at Ramadan
The tiny little murmurs of my baby sister
Smooth-centred Galaxy dissolving on my tongue
The soft sound of *tap, tap, tap,* from the feet of a tap dancer.

The sweet song of a bluebird sitting merrily on a branch
I'm sitting on the top of the mountain, in the North Pole
Feeling the sharp icy breeze on my cheeks
I will be surfing on top of the seven-coloured rainbow.

The rustles and dropping of autumn leaves on the wet pavement
The noisy bellowing, lecturing voice of a teacher, captured
in a fishing net

My box is fashioned with ice crystals and multicoloured diamonds
In the edges it has the most sweet laughter of every baby in the world
My box is fashioned like a glamorous swan with glistening wings!

Kolchuma Begum (12)
Walshaw High School

Morning

Morning comes with curtains drawing
Morning comes with a bright sun shining
Morning comes with an alarm clock ringing
Morning comes with the milkman whistling
Morning comes with the radio blaring
Morning comes with dogs barking.

Shannon Bythell (11)
Walshaw High School

The Pakistan Earthquake

Many people losing lives
Losing children, husbands and wives
The earthquake destroyed it all
Aid being sent by the people need more
Many injured, so much pain
Hoping that it doesn't happen again
Money is being sent
And people giving love
Rebuilding lives
Back to how they should
Before it was a happy place
Children playing, hear their cheers
Now there is sadness
Crying and tears.

Carly Law (13)
Walshaw High School

Friendships

Friends will come,
Friends will go,
The seasons change,
But our friendship will stay,
Strong and true.

I believe in angels,
The kind that Heaven sends,
I'm surrounded by angels,
But I call them . . . *friends!*

Friendship is like a breeze,
You can't hold it,
Smell it,
Taste it,
But you can feel it,
It's a wonderful feeling!

Henna Ali (12)
Walshaw High School

The Meaning Of Love

Love is meaning what you say
Love is caring whatever the day
Love is blinding but also so clear
Love is something never to fear.

Love is calm
Love is concern
Love is unconditional
But also stern.

Love has feelings
Love has admiration
Love has meaning
As well as attraction.

Love needs affection
Love needs passion
Love needs desire
Almost like me.

Salma Hanif (15)
Walshaw High School

Vision

I sit there listening,
I may not see,
But I too have hears, quite evidently.

I hear you giggling,
I may not see,
But I too have feelings, quite surprisingly.

I sense the closeness,
I may not see,
But I do want the distance between you and me.

I feel you touch me,
I may not see,
But I too have a fist, quite reluctantly.

Maria Ali (15)
Walshaw High School

Worried

I am worried, what shall I do?

My secrets will get revealed,
One by one they will all get peeled,
My happiness will be snatched away,
What shall I say?

I am worried, what shall I do?

In my family, problems will arise,
Why do I have a feeling someone dies?
What kind of feeling is this?
What have I missed?

I am worried, what shall I do?

My family is crying,
I feel like dying,
What kind of life have I got?
I wish I just got shot!

Hafsa Bibi (12)
Walshaw High School

Why?

Why do trees whistle in the wind?
Aren't children supposed to do that?
Why do the flowers sing and dance?
Do they have feelings? Who will ever know?
Why is there sorrow? Why is there pain?
The feeling of death? Outside in the rain.
Why is there money?
What is the point?
It has caused so many problems . . .
It has caused so many tears . . .
Why all these questions?
Why all these thoughts?
None ever to be answered . . . why?

Grace Pickering (13)
Walshaw High School

The Peace Box

(Based on 'Magic Box' by Kit Wright)

I will put in my box . . .
A drop of water from the Lake District,
The texts from my dad each morning,
The scent of Angel perfume on Paula.

I will put in my box . . .
The sound of a baby laughing,
The photo of my mum, dad and sister together
And the taste of Galaxy chocolate, smooth and silky.

I will put in my box . . .
The feel of silk on my skin,
The smile of my mum,
The touch of my sister's hand.

I will put in the peace box . . .
The hills from Hurstwood,
The last holiday with my mum and dad together,
The cross from my dear nana.

I shall place in the box . . .
A school full of stars
And a sky full of children.
My sister's first laugh
And the hug from my granny,
The warm, comforting hug.

I shall use my box . . .
To remember the past,
Not to re-live it,
But just to sit and view it.
Sit in my nana's back garden,
Eating chocolate ice cream,
While laughing!

Amilia Crossley (12)
Walshaw High School

My Allah

Oh Allah, I look to You to guide me in life,
Help me through this journey,
Let me be a good Muslim . . .
Day and night.

Help me to obey You in every sense
Let the angels come, which You have sent.
Creator of everything beautiful,
As a Muslim, let my duties be fulfilled.

Help me to be a good person,
Help me to do what's right,
Help me to have devotion,
Help me to live peacefully in life.

When my time is over,
When my life comes to an end,
Help me to be prepared,
In every single sense.

When Judgement Day is here,
Forgive me for all my sins,
Let me have no fear,
In Your paradise, let me in.

Allah, I ask You, to help me through life,
Allah, I ask You, to stay by my side,
Allah, I ask You, to protect me on this Earth,
Allah, I ask You, bless the woman who to me, gave birth.

Your Blessed Name is kept deep within my heart,
Of your Holy religion, I am a part,
Islam is a gift which You have sent,
Let all the angels from Heaven, to Earth descend,
Thank You Allah, for giving me life,
Thank You Allah, for every star in the sky!

Badeea Qureshi (14)
Walshaw High School

Ghost Recipe

Ingredients
One adult
One haunted house
One clock striking midnight
Three school children
Two pints of blood
Four rotten fingers
A scream
Four skeletons
Guts of a frozen pig
Twelve fresh horses' eyeballs.

Method
Simply take one adult
And put it in a haunted house.
Leave for 15 minutes to get scared.
Add the sound of a clock striking midnight.
Take three children and add two pints of blood.

Sprinkle four rotten fingers.
When terrified, scream at the top of your voice.
Leave to simmer for half-an-hour.
While you mix up a brew of four skeletons,
With gut of a pig that's frozen.

Serve with twelve freshly picked eyeballs.

Now enjoy, if you dare!

Aimee Duckworth (13)
Walshaw High School

Untitled

A world, a whole new world:
Fantasy is reality in a strange atmosphere
A deep waterfall of colour comes slowly down
Magic, spirits, creatures and uninvented images
Is in a world of imagination.

A world, a whole magic world:
Twinkling specks among spoken spells
The fire burning within a dragon
A crescent moon and stars on a wizard's cloak
Is in a world of imagination.

A world, a whole evil world:
The blood-red sharp reflection of evil in devil's eyes
The music and life of 'rock'
Gothic crosses, skulls and the black nothingness
Is in a world of imagination.

A world, a whole happy world:
Flying high with a pair of bird's delicate wings
Flowers covering green grass in fields
Fairies, pixies and little animals
All in a world of imagination.

A world, a whole different world:
Filled with the power of my imagination
Dreams great and strong spring to mind
Thoughts never heard of in all mankind!

Eleanor Greenwood (12)
Walshaw High School

Friends Are . . .

Friends are treasures
That stay in the sea and come to the surface
When you need help
They never let a tear drop from your eye
Without being there.

Friends are keys
To our hearts, they unlock our happiness
And give us joy.

Friends are the sun
That shines on you
They give you comfort and keep you safe.

Friends look over you
They never turn their back
They are there all the time
In our dreams, hopes and wishes.

Raisah Ahmed (12)
Walshaw High School

Yellow

Yellow is . . .
Sunshine on a warm summer day,
A shooting star across a pitch-black sky,
'The Simpsons' on a flickering, colour TV,
A rubber duck bobbing in the bath,
The fresh, new smell of spring.

Yellow is . . .
Tall sunflowers reaching for the sky,
The happy, smiling face of a joyful child,
Bees covered in a dusting of pollen,
A lone buttercup in the grass,
Lions cubs playing in the dust.

Elesha McWilliam (13)
Walshaw High School

I Shall Put In My Box . . .

(Based on 'Magic Box' by Kit Wright)

I shall put in my box . . .
The first time I had chocolate, smooth or rough
When my sister gave me a piggyback, running, jumping and laughing
When I went on holiday, swimming in the cold, refreshing pool

I shall put in my box . . .
When I first got my horse, riding, trotting, cantering and galloping
When I first had a snowball fight, freezing cold with shivering hands.

I shall put in my box . . .
When I got my dogs and cats,
Taking them for walks in the rustling grass
When I had hot chips for tea, tasting the softness of them.

I shall put in my box . . .
When I moved from Burnley to Padiham, looking out at the field
When I got my favourite ornament, putting it on my window sill.

I shall put in my box . . .
When I moved to Walshaw High School
Scary and frightening
From getting lost to getting used to it!

Charlotte Lord (12)
Walshaw High School

Autumn

Autumn is an explosion of ancient colours,
Hot apple pie on a cold night,
An ocean of leaves, bombarding the streets.
Whistle of the wind through the trees,
The screeching of fireworks repeating every night,
Autumn is the season of beautiful sights
Views, smells and touch.

Elizabeth Davis (13)
Walshaw High School

A Friend

A friend is a precious pearl,
That is always with you.

A friend is a priceless gift,
That you can never find easily.

A friend will always be there for you,
Even if the world is against you.

A friend will always care and like you,
Even if you split up.

A friend is a wonderful treasure,
That is locked up in your heart.

A friend is something wonderful,
That is attached to your memory.

A friend is a lovely and harmless mark,
That is on your soul forever!

A friend is a great companion,
That leads you to the right path.

A friend will give you fragrance,
That will stay at one corner of your heart.

Friendship is a key to happiness,
That brings you to another world.

Saadia Ramzan (13)
Walshaw High School

The Heart Of The Ocean

You remind me of the heart of the ocean,
Lonely and abandoned,
Waiting to be found again,
Like a small child lost in a crowd
With your head lowly bowed,
You remind me of the heart of the ocean.

Heidi Louise Brooker (15)
Walshaw High School

Love Is . . .

A bed made of roses
An exploding heart
A red sea of emotion
Weak at the knees
A room full of joy and happiness
A box of treasured memories
A river of peace flowing through your heart
A land where dreams come true.

Love is . . .
Like the molecules of oxygen
The gentle breeze of the sea
A handful of freshly picked flowers
A moment that lasts forever
A blazing flame, golden and full of warmth
A piece of art, so beautiful and valuable
The key that unlocks the gates of Heaven
The greatest smile.

Love is . . .
The best thing that can ever happen to you.

Chelsea Joanna Sagar (13)
Walshaw High School

Chocolate

I am sweet and creamy
And very, very dreamy,
When you're upset,
I am your comfort.
I am your friend,
Your only weakness.
Melting on your tongue,
Giving a sweet sensation,
No one can resist
The irresistible temptation.

Aisha Tahir (14)
Walshaw High School

My Memory

My grandad - in my memory I will keep:
The sound of his laughter beating against my ears
The soft deep sensation of his voice approaching my ears
The smell of the tobacco from the hookah going up my nose
The light innocent eyes of my grandad watching me play.

My grandma - in my memory I will keep:
The smile on her face when she saw I had arrived back from school
The mitai she gave me melting in my mouth
Her soft voice, calling me, echoing in my mind
The dark beautiful eyes of my grandma watching me play.

Mehack Zareen (12)
Walshaw High School

Anger Is . . .

Anger is . . .
A roar of fire
A bursting balloon
A crocodile cry
What can we do?

Anger is . . .
Love turning to hatred
Anger rotating into frustration
A pot of stone cold blood
What can we do?

Anger is . . .
Sunshine fading away
Darkness taking over
Heart burning with no sympathy.

Don't take things to heart,
You never know what it can turn into.

Fatima Hussain (12)
Walshaw High School

The Magic Box

(Based on 'Magic Box' by Kit Wright)

I will put in my box . . .
The ray of the sun on a hot morning
The sun bright as ever, when it's midday
The last ray of the sun dawning.

I will put in my box . . .
The sound of a baby's first laugh
The Earth slowly spinning
The sun turning into the moon.

I will put in my box . . .
The smell of the first rose after April showers
The crunch of autumn leaves
The smell of rain.

I will put in my box . . .
An Indian woman dancing merrily
People singing Christmas carols
The rush of water at Niagara Falls.

My box is made from . . .
The harshest substance on Earth - diamond
With brilliant glistening golden stars
With hidden secrets.

As soon as I open my box . . .
My dead grandma's soul touches my face
My happy memories come to life again and again.

Saira Hassan (12)
Walshaw High School

Winter!

Winter is white like a blanket of snow
It smells like freshly baked apple pie
It tastes like a warm Sunday roast
It looks like a red robin snuggled in its nest
It feels like sitting round a fire with your family eating sweets!

Amy Howarth (13)
Walshaw High School

Oh Calculator

Oh calculator, you are such a clever clogs,
You are as easy as playing pogs.
You make things easier for everyone,
You start as easy as one plus one.

You can do long sums,
Better than human's mums.
You always win the race of sums,
You never lose to a human.

Food we need to eat to get moving,
Batteries you need to get working.
We need you to get our answers correct,
Otherwise we might fail our tests.

Pakeezah Younis (12)
Walshaw High School

South Asia Earthquake!

Life was like paradise,
Children playing here and there,
Mothers cooking special meals
And fathers laying the tables with care.
Then all of a sudden, the earth was shaking,
Mothers, fathers and children were scared,
The house had gone, the quake took everything away,
There was nothing left, everyone was dead!
The happy times we had together,
They've all faded away,
We have lost our loved ones, the ones we loved the most,
But now they are not here, not even today,
Oh God, bring back our lives,
The ones we had before this,
We need help, we need comfort,
Now we can't even give our children
A goodnight kiss!

Aisha Shakir (13)
Walshaw High School

Autumn Is . . .

Giving things to other people and thinking about older people
The weather starts to change hot, cold to snow
The crunchy, crispy leaves falling off the huge trees
Hallowe'en children trick or treating
Conkers dropping from the trees and surrounding the base and roots
Fireworks exploding in the night air
Red, yellow and orange, multicoloured and bright.

Tahmina Ahmed (12)
Walshaw High School

The Mysterious Box

(Based on 'Magic Box' by Kit Wright)

In the box I will put . . .
A plate of stars
A sky of sweets
The children waiting for it to all fall down.

In the box I will put . . .
My friends who are very keen
To have their belly buttons pierced
Are all what I need
Because they're just like me.

In the box I will put . . .
Baby's cute, adoring face
Ready to smile
But struggling to smile
And starting to cry!

In the box I will put . . .
The smell of cooking
Ready to open, your fast
Ready to read the prayer
Ready to go to *sleep* . . .

Homara Ilyas (13)
Walshaw High School

Fame Isn't Everything!

There are so many famous people in the world,
Some are boys and some are girls.
Some were famous right from the start,
Landing them with a big part.

Brad Pitt has often been told,
If he made it to sixty, he'll get extra gold.
It is a fact that wealthy men,
Like extra gold, now and then.

Britney Spears could sing and dance,
Lately she was offered a chance.
To start her own family,
One man chose her especially.

Tom Cruise has become an action hero,
I bet his role model was Robert De Niro.
Tom Cruise has starred in Mission Impossible,
The events that happened were quite possible.

J-Lo is a singer and an actress,
She starred in many films without making a fuss.
Not many people get the chance,
To sing, act or dance.

James Bond is his name,
Fighting evil is his game.
Pretty women in his bed,
Turn against him and you're dead.

All these stars are the same,
The pressure builds from all the fame.
They do a lot of things they regret,
Which is very hard to forget.

A moral is what this poem brings,
Fame isn't everything!

Nosheen Begum (14)
Walshaw High School

My Precious Box

(Based on 'Magic Box' by Kit Wright)

I will put in the box . . .
My elegant, white gold jewellery
Japanese birds speaking English on a misty night
And the first word my brother said.

I will put in the box . . .
The happiness in my family
The purple sky
And the two moons.

I will put in the box . . .
The bell that goes at ten past three
The laughter at the school fields
And the last chat with an ancient uncle.

I will put in the box . . .
The atmosphere on my sister's wedding
The tenth planet, orange and pink
A cow looking down at the moon
And the moon gazing up at the cow.

My box is decorated from the clouds
The sun and the moon
With the rain on the lid and snow on the lock
And all of my secrets covered in frost.

I'm gonna sail on this box
To the middle of nowhere.
Where I can meet
Tony Bush and George Blair!

Shabnam Farah (13)
Walshaw High School

Lion Cub

They have left me here in a cage,
On my own,
In a cage.
They have taken me away from my family,
In the wild
And put me in a cage.
There's others,
In cages,
Animals,
Monkeys, giraffes, elephants
And me.
Why have they done this?
I never did anything to these people.
They are surrounding me,
Staring at me.

They have put me in a cage.

Elisha Moore (13)
Walshaw High School

Sat In A Café

A girl sat in a café
Eating worms with white teeth
Her jet-black hair
Falls around her head like a sheath
Eating tea and biscuits
She looks like she is a shark
He slices the ham as he watches
Her coat, her lips, her eyeshade, all very dark
A very bright light shines
Eating in front of the young man
A conversation in the background
The biscuit still in her hand.

Bakhtaawer Malik (12)
Walshaw High School

If Only You Knew How Much I Loved You

It has taken years for us to meet,
From the moment I set my eyes on you, I marked you to be mine,
Your presence drives me crazy, I can't think straight,
I placed you on my eyelashes,
So you were always in my dreams forever,
I'm wounded by your love, that's what makes me act the way I do,
I spend sleepless nights, counting the stars in the sky,
I chose one to be yours,
Our hearts mixed into one colour,
I couldn't tell which of me was you and which of you was me.

Now, I can see which of me was you and which of you was me,
We stand so close, yet we are so far,
You always learnt how to break my heart,
But never did you learn to fix the pieces back together again,
I gave you so many chances,
But never did you learn from your mistakes,
My heart feels empty without you,
I told you to stay,
But you carried on walking and you didn't ever look back once.

If only you knew how much I loved you!

Atikah Parveen (12)
Walshaw High School

Happiness

Happiness is yellow like the golden sun
It tastes like marshmallows warmed on a hot BBQ
It smells like grass that's just been cut
It looks like butter melting on hot crispy toast
It sounds like birds singing in the morning
It feels like falling into a bed of cotton wool.

Sarah Hayhurst (15)
Walshaw High School

The Earthquake

Thousands have died
Millions are injured.
They are asking for help,
What shall we do?

Thousands have died,
Millions are injured.
Children without parents
And parents without children.
What shall we do?

Thousands have died,
Millions are injured.
Some need homes,
Some need food.
What shall we do?

Thousands have died,
Millions are injured.
The buildings have fallen,
The people are trapped.
What shall we do?

Thousands have died,
Millions are injured.
Waiting for help,
But none is coming.
What did you do?

Shazia Waheed (12)
Walshaw High School

The Magic Keyhole

Looking through the keyhole I can see . . .
A mystical sandstorm of feathers
A waterfall of a golden phoenix
A box of baby rabbits
A rainbow smile across my house.

Whilst looking through the keyhole I can see . . .
A butterfly spreading its wings
A spoonful of chocolate river
A broad smile across my face
An opening to a promised land.

Whilst looking through the keyhole I can see . . .
A teenager's first kiss
The sun setting for the day
A quick hug from my friends.

Whilst looking through the keyhole I can see . . .
My sister's welcoming smile
My parents' goodnight hug
My grandma's sweet hello
My grandad's cheerful wave.

Whilst looking through the keyhole I hope to see . . .
Wedding bells and a sandy beach
A share of success
A feeling of love forever.

Libby Pickering (13)
Walshaw High School

Autumn Is . . .

Autumn is . . .
A bed of leaves
A vast expanse of colours, saffron, vermilion, auburn
A streaky, overhead light lighting up our homes
The rattle of windows escaping howling wind.

Autumn is . . .
A crackle of a raging fire
A bang of a Catherine wheel, illuminating the sky
Witches chanting on broomsticks
The evil glow of a pumpkin grinning maliciously.

Autumn is . . .
The *chingle-changle* of bangles
The dancing feet of families
The fairy light twinkling in the distance
The tinkling of clashing glasses.

Autumn is a portrait of multicoloured trees
Swaying to the rhythm of the wind.

Masooma Begum (13)
Walshaw High School

English

E nglish, I don't like that much
N ot at all to be honest, but
G ive me less writing
L et's make it exciting and
I might just enjoy myself
S o stop the
H omework!

Cos we're tired!

Hafssah Sajid
Walshaw High School

The Feeling Of Christmas!

Christmas is . . .
The snow, white like fresh paper,
Cold, icy air running down your throat,
Snowflakes on the floor, just waiting to melt,
Bright lights, brightening up the city streets,
Decorations all over like a rainbow-coloured picture,
Stars in the sky, shining bright to bring a twinkle to the land,
Mistletoe above the door, waiting to be christened,
Celebrations across the country, songs, dancing and more,
The tinkling of the bells on Santa's sleigh,
Children walking up at 7 o'clock in the morning,
Listening to the low rustle of the tiny feet running down the stairs,
The smell of a warm roast turkey, ready to eat,
The joy of opening gifts on *that day!*
The look on their faces like you have just saved the day,
Christmas is Christmas and that's the way it's going to stay!

Maxine Louise Brierley (13)
Walshaw High School

My Precious Box

(Based on 'Magic Box' by Kit Wright)

In my box I would put . . .
A precious smile from a friend
A cosy hug from a mum
A friend getting angry.

In my box I would put . . .
The crunchy autumn leaves rustling on the floor
My first birthday when I was three
Walking in the green field by myself.

In my box I would put . . .
When I stepped into the magical world of Camelot with my friends
A beautiful necklace that my best friend put around my neck
When I smelt the fragrance Gucci Rush 2.

Mokiete Munawar (12)
Walshaw High School

Winter Is . . .

A coat of glazing frost on the ground
Lots of people loading a trolley until it's jam-packed
People wearing woolly hats,
Warm scarves and soft gloves,
Children playing snowball fights,
Maybe breaking people's windows
Rosy cheeks when cold outside,
Slippery ice for everyone to fall down,
The astonished faces when snow falls down softly.

Winter is . . .
The warm glow of getting to spend time with your family
Frosty trees heavy with glowing snow,
Skidding across the ice and skating with your friends
A time of celebration for lots of religions.

Masuma Begum (12)
Walshaw High School

Autumn

Autumn is . . .
A blanket of leaves
A flowing stream of colours
A carpet of crunchy noises
A rainfall of leaves
An explosion of a firework
A trick or treater
A darkness creeping upon us
A sharp bitterness in the air
A bare forest, but
A season of fun.

Cara Johnson (13)
Walshaw High School

Rain Is . . .

Rain is . . .
A vast of unwanted flood
The violent storm, lashing the sky
Destruction, damage.

Rain is . . .
Tiny droplets gathering on a leaf
A puddle to jump in with wellies.

Rain is . . .
An April silver shower, sparkling in the sun,
A beautiful rainbow arched in the sky.

Rain is . . .
The gentle pitter-patter on the windowpane
A sea of umbrellas.

Mariam Yousaf (12)
Walshaw High School

Shattered

Shattered is silver like a frozen lake
It tastes like old ice frappe
It smells like ash and burning ambers
It looks like shards of coloured glass
It sounds like a mirror broken into splinters
It feels like a bag of broken biscuits.

Sownia Ramzan (13)
Walshaw High School

Peace Is . . .

Peace is the silence of a baby sleeping
Peace is the spring lamb leaping
Peace is a soft white feather landing neatly
Peace is the rough sea crashing at a wall
Peace is the snowflakes that fall
Peace is needed around the world
Peace is the wish of every boy and girl
Peace is like a precious pearl.

I pray for peace.

Christina Rachel Howard (13)
Walshaw High School

Autumn - Haiku

Autumn has arrived
Leaves are falling from the trees
Reds, greens and yellows.

Jessica Elizabeth Neary (12)
Walshaw High School

Excitement

Excitement is colourful like rainbows in the sky
It tastes like different flavoured sweets
It smells like doughnuts straight from the oven
It looks like presents at Christmas
It sounds like a bonfire crackling in the dark
It feels like riding a roller coaster.

Lauren Collinge (13)
Walshaw High School

In The Mansion

In the mansion,
After a long journey,
The bang of the windows,
The chuckle of water,
The attic chattering,
Making the door squeak,
The flames are roaring,
The ghost in the air,
Making the curtains shiver,
The echoes from the kitchen,
The books flying,
The blood in the drawer,
Trickling down,
The skeleton in the cupboard,
Hanging like a bat,
The graveyard is haunting,
The mansion cries every night,
No one knows why,
The dark queen comes
And makes everything silent . . .

Jaida Begum (11)
Walshaw High School

Winter Poem

W et strong winds, furiously blowing around
I cy bitter frost covering the ground
N ew Year's Eve parties being planned
T easing snowflakes drifting down
E nchanting decorations and festive food
R eceiving and giving presents.

Amy Longworth (13)
Walshaw High School

My Fantasy Box

(Based on 'Magic Box' by Kit Wright)

In my fantasy box I will put . . .
The leaves changing colour in autumn
The buds on the trees in spring
The snow falling softly in winter
The colourful flowers in summer.

In my fantasy box I will put . . .
My final conversation with my grandad
The experience of my first pantomime
The final at Blackpool Tower ballroom
The last days in Year 6.

In my fantasy box I will put . . .
Lots of beautiful things
My dancing dress
My jewellery
My photos
And the glowing moon.

In my fantasy box I will put . . .
The smiles of my friends
A brilliant book
The pumpkins on Hallowe'en
The presents at Christmas.

My box will be made of . . .
All of my memories bonded together
Autumn leaves
Cats' whiskers
Happy times.

Hannah Roberts (14)
Walshaw High School

Would You?

If I were to cry,
Would you cry with me too?
Would you do more than try?
Would you always be true?

Would you sing when I'm sad?
Would you be my best mate?
Would you be calm when I'm mad
Or would you yell when I'm late?

If I were to sing,
Would you hate that song?
Would you let your mood swing
Or would you just sing-a-long?

Would you laugh when I'm funny
Or pretend you like my jokes?
Would you just want my money?
Would you try avoiding my folks?

If I said I love you,
Would you say you loved me?
Would you pretend to
Or just ignore me?

Would you ever want to leave?
Am I enough to miss?
Do you want a second to breathe
So that you can answer all this?

Zayanah Mansor (14)
Walshaw High School

At The Bakery

'Hello my dear, what would you like?'
'Two cheese and onion pasties please.'

'A cherry bake with some banana milkshake?'
'No, just two cheese and onion pasties please.'

'A hard boiled egg with some toast?'
'No thank you, just two cheese and onion pasties please.'

'Two bread rolls and meatballs?'
'No, no, no, just two cheese and onion pasties please.'

'Chocolate fudge cake, you get two for the price of one?'
'No, no, no, I just want two cheese and onion pasties, all right?'

'Oh I am truly sorry my dear, we didn't make any pasties this year!'

'Grr . . . !'

Ridah Jamil (12)
Walshaw High School

Autumn

Leaves twirling whirling all around
Falling down to the ground.

Children playing having fun
In the light of the setting sun.

A sea of colours red, brown and gold
On the trees that are getting old.

Conkers dropping off the trees
Knocking down all the leaves.

I hear fireworks go *bang!*
As the children sing . . . *'Trick or treat?'*

Alison Burrows (13)
Walshaw High School